P9-DNJ-064

This is
DIVING

This is
DIVING

A Complete
Underwater Course

DUILIO MARCANTE

SECOND EDITION

SHERIDAN HOUSE

Contributors: Alberto Azzali, Sergio Canu, Paolo Colantoni, Enzo Dagnino, Luigi Ferraro (Vice-President C.M.A.S.), Gianni Foroni, Sebastiano Gugliemo, Hermann Heberlein, Giulio E. Melegari, Giorgio Odaglia, Gian Carlo Ricci, Giuseppe Viotti, Damiano Zanini.
Photography: Enzo Bottesini, Giancarlo Annunziata, Gisella and Gianni Beltrami, Sergio Canu, Paolo Curto, Paolo Ferraro, Renato Idra, Franco La Penna, Francesco Lo Savio, Angela Macaluso, Giulio E. Melegari, Giuseppe Merlo, Francesco Pugliese, Luigi Rossato, Claudio Sorrenti, Armando Tommei, Pierfranco Dilenge, Enrico Gargiulo, Sergio Loppel, Gino Catalucci, Maurizio Fossati.
Revised by Remo Trucchi

Technical editor, first English edition: Mike Busuttili

Revised U.S. edition edited by Jeannine Simon

Copyright © United Nautical Publishers SA, Basel 1989

First edition 1976

This edition first published
in the United States of America 1989 by
Sheridan House Inc.
145 Palisade Street
Dobbs Ferry, NY 10522

ISBN 0 911378 96 0

Printed in Italy.

Contents

3725

Preface

Diving is a young sport, just a few decades old, but experiencing rapid growth as more and more people are introduced to the wonders of the underwater world. The pioneers of the sport faced many unknown dangers in their early adventures but the present day diver has the benefit of well developed techniques, extensive medical research, and modern equipment all contributing to make recreational diving safe and enjoyable.

Man's new familiarity with the sea has taught him far more about life under the sea and about the delicate balance which nature maintains between the species found there. He has progressed from his earlier position as hunter, often killing fish unnecessarily, to a more responsible participation concerned with maintaining the balance of underwater life and conserving its benefits for those who will come after him.

Modern techniques and teaching methods can now ensure that almost anyone can learn to dive in complete safety and to master the latest equipment which minimizes the risk of accident and maximizes the chances of overcoming any incident.

This book provides a clear and accurate introduction to the techniques of diving and their scientific basis. It is especially intended for the beginner, indicating the scope of his initial exploration and the range of activities open to him as he gathers skill and experience. The advice we give is based on practical experience in teaching beginners and a knowledge of their needs. We do not suggest nor recommend that the reader sets out to teach herself or himself to dive on the basis of the advice we give here. The guidance of a qualified instructor is essential for the safe transition from novice to experienced diver. To plunge in is easy but to dive well is to have a clear understanding of all the physical and physiological phenomena which affect diving and to stay within the limits which they impose.

As the diver gains experience, the aspects of safety become more automatic and routine and more attention can be given to the pleasures of diving: the thrill of exploration, the wonder of nature, the enjoyment of a new medium, the contrast with everyday life, the relaxation of a sport fully enjoyed and mastered.

This illustrated diving manual was originally written in Italian by Diulio Marcante who is known the world over for his experience in the field. He has assembled a team of experts, well-known instructors, technicians and physicians. The new edition covers the latest techniques and equipment, in a field where the Italian participation is in the vanguard. Many full-color illustrations have been added.

The book should be kept handy as a reference source and to remind the less experienced divers of the universally recommended techniques. Addresses for contacting recommended teaching organizations and clubs are given at the end.

Introduction

Life below the surface

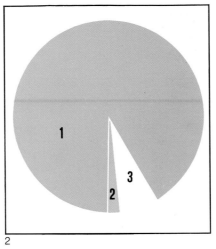

2

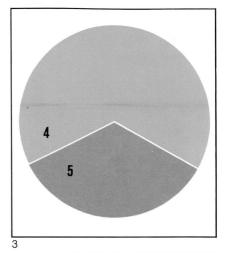

3

Air and Sea

Seven-tenths of the surface of the globe is covered with water, and this is the reason for the sea being the main constituent of life on this planet (figure 3). Man effectively occupies only the dry land, but depends on water for almost all his food, energy, commerce, industry etc. Of the water in the world the proportions of sea (1) lakes and rivers (2) and ice (3) are shown in figure 2.

By his nature man has remained earthbound, so much so that to become moderately proficient in swimming techniques, and then to learn to dive, has taken him millions of years of evolution. He has also realized that certain phenomena to which he was accustomed in the open air have very different values underwater. The principal differences are as follows:

The slowing down of movements
Rapid loss of temperature
Reduction in light intensity
Differences in refraction and
reflection
Altered acoustics
Large changes in pressure for
relatively small changes in depth.

All this is due to the fact that water compared with the atmosphere is 800 times denser, and 60 times more viscous. Also, in water, the speed of transmission of light is reduced to one-third, but that of sound is five times greater.

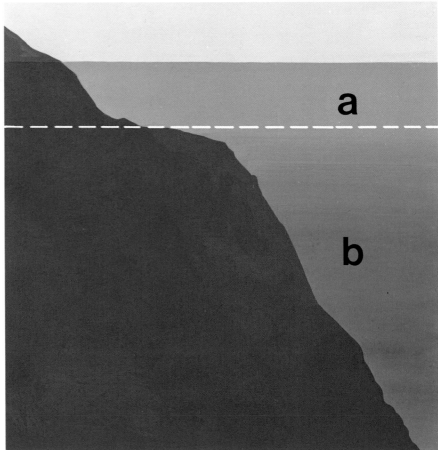

a

b

4

These effects are universal so that wherever man confronts the underwater world, in the oceans, inland seas, underwater lakes, or turbulent rivers, the conditions he finds are the same. They may vary to some extent depending on temperature and whether the water is cloudy or salty, but the differences compared with life in the atmosphere are always considerable.

In the marine world each zone, each geographical area, each individual site, and each particular depth has variations in fauna and flora peculiar to itself. Man has so far learnt little of all this; only the small and restricted upper layer has up to now been the object of direct and systematic research (4-a).

This zone, which is so insignificant in relation to the vast total underwater volume, is none the less the one which contains by far the greatest part of the marvelous variety of marine life. This is because most living organisms in the sea depend on light. As the light diminishes and gradually fades into an ever denser purple gloom, vegetable life ceases and even its simplest forms disappear. This occurs, not at extreme depths, but at only a few hundred feet (4-b).

Water acts as a selective filter which progressively absorbs the various components of white light or sunlight as the depth increases. Upon descending one notices that red is the first to disappear, then orange, yellow, green and finally blue as it merges into darker and darker tones of purple at the maximum depth that light can penetrate below the sea. (5).

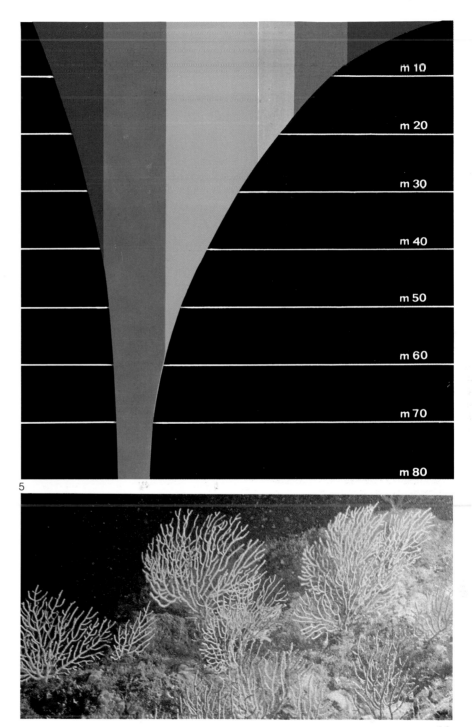

5

m 10

m 20

m 30

m 40

m 50

m 60

m 70

m 80

6 *Gorgonian at 20 meters.*

7 *Eel grass (Posidonia).*

8 *A Mediterranean reef.*

9 *A coral reef.*

Underwater life

Marine growth has become adapted over millions of years to the reduced light and establishes itself on the reefs along the shoreline, covering the rocks, submerged piles of stones, wrecks and any other objects that fall to the sea bottom. Some varieties, such as kelp, form dense forests, which at times can grow thirty meters or more before reaching the surface of the sea. Growth of this type is often found near the coasts of California, Argentina, Chile, Peru and New Zealand.

Another example, the sargasso weed, has developed bladders filled with air which keep it afloat, so that its movement depends on the action of the winds and currents. It is typical of a particular area of the Atlantic which is known, in fact, as the Sargasso Sea.

Elsewhere, in the Mediterranean and along the southern coast of Australia, as well as varieties of seaweed, the diver encounters strange fields formed of a higher type of plant, the bottle-green eel grass (*posidonia*). This grows in ribbons along the coast line to depths of about thirty meters (7).

In the sea, it can be said with certainty, that where there is vegetation there is also animal life. Life is also abundant in the vast sandy expanses of the shallow offshore waters of many low lying coasts, as well as around shallow reefs.

Animal life even appears out of apparently deserted depths where reefs project slightly from the sea. In such cases it is the solid support that is provided by the rocks which appeals to the variety of living forms which accumulate and pile one upon the other, until often they end up as an incrustation several centimeters thick on whose surface thousands of minute animals live and die (9).

Sponges, both common and calcareous, star fish (11), *alcionari, madrepores,* shellfish, tube worms, crustaceans and

10 *Queen Angel fish.*

11 *Starfish.*

12 *Tropical Madrepore*

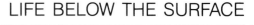

13 *Red Coral (Mediterranean).*

14 *Gorgonian.*

15 *Rose coral.*

seaweeds appear before the eyes of the diver on every square centimeter of the rocky walls. In the right conditions branches of coral weave a pattern of colors, which in spite of its seeming confusion, is nevertheless natural and harmonious.

Sandbanks and sunken reefs can extend from considerable depths to reach the surface of the water or a few feet above it. They are oases of swarming life over which hover shoals of fish both local and migratory. Just looking at such sights is enough to satisfy most divers.

In the warm climates near the tropics there are islands of calcareous rock which

are composed of the shells and skeletons of millions of marine animals and vast quantities of coral producing madrepores. Typical of very saline waters are the islands of the Red Sea, and also the atolls of the Pacific. The latter are often formed from submerged volcanoes, and consist of a circular calcareous ring, with a lagoon in the center, which may or may not have openings to the sea. Such islands are multicolored living platforms formed by the continuous work of millions of *polyps* or *madrepores.*

Marine animals, like corals which build deposits, or like molluscs which form shells, use considerable quantities of car-

bonates of calcium and magnesium, which reduce the amounts of these two salts that are present in solution in the sea. Ordinary sea water contains about 30 grams of common salt for every liter. This average value is reduced in cool water, such as the Baltic which can only hold about 10 grams, and is increased in warm water, such as the Red Sea which has up to 43 grams per liter. Exceptionally high values are reached in enclosed waters and lagoons.

Salinity is directly proportional to density; so much so that man is able to float much more easily in the sea than in a lake or river.

16 *A Mediterranean reef.*

17 *Gorgonian.*

18 *Cup corals.*

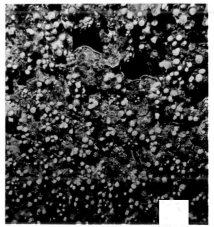

Conservation of the environment

The seas and oceans are mankind's greatest source of food and materials, which consist of fish, many types of animals, seaweeds, salts for varied uses including sodium chloride, magnesium and potassium. There are also minerals of industrial importance such as manganese, animal and vegetable substances for pharmaceutical use, for example ambergris from sperm whales, and iodine from brown seaweed. The sea is also the object of thoughtless destructive activity (19, 20, 21, 22).

The rivers of the industrialized countries carry into the sea daily thousands of tons of solid and liquid waste, which spreads out and affects the environmental balance, and causes grave danger to animal and vegetable life. Those who are able to dive into this undersea world can appreciate its fascination today because it is still alive. But the deterioration in the last decades has been so great that those who saw it then are appalled to think of what it will be like in the future if the present rate of pollution continues.

In the face of impending disaster the conservation of the environment, which a few years ago was looked upon merely as being morally and ethically desirable, is today linked closely to the future survival of the human species.

When one remembers that a man can survive for 30 days without food, for three days without water, but not even three minutes without oxygen, one can well understand that the need to fight against pollution is absolutely vital.

The sport and profession of diving is on the increase everywhere, and it is the duty of each diver to work for this cause which is essential for the common good. It is a struggle that humanity must direct against itself, against its own system of living, and against the very civilization which it has built up and which it can so easily destroy.

19 *Pollution from rubbish.*

20 *Pollution from smoke.*

21 *Pollution from wreckage.*

CONSERVATION OF THE ENVIRONMENT

It is a struggle that must be directed first against pollution which is the greatest danger, against the great industrial fisheries equipped with water pumps to suck up from the depths whole shoals of fish, against certain types of professional fishing, and against the poachers who work more often than not with explosives.

Underwater sport fishing and hunting should be better controlled, though at present the damage that is done by these means is relatively small. In practice it is restricted to the permanent local species which form part of the diver's underwater scene, and not to the deep-sea fish which provide the majority of our food stocks.

Even if we manage to avoid poisoning the sea we will still have to look after the control and re-population of the oceans. Indispensable in this aim is the provision of many protected zones, the so called 'Marine Parks'. These must not be thought of only as sub-aqua playgrounds, but essentially areas for looking after and maintaining an underwater environment, for studying the conservation of sea life, and for the education of tomorrow's users of the oceans.

23 *The beauty of a coral reef.*

24 *A snorkeler searching a cave.*

25 26 *In the underwater parks fish can become extremely tame.*

PART

1

Medical and Scientific Aspects of Diving

Some basic physics

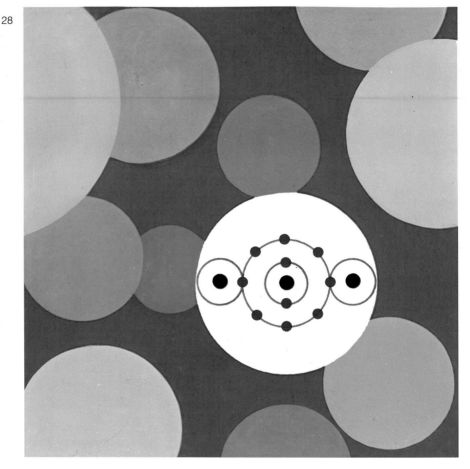

When venturing under water, man has to modify some of his normal instincts which could cause reactions that would be disastrous for him in this new environment. To learn these safeguards he must know something of the laws of physics and of the make-up of the human body when surrounded by this medium.

He must have a complete knowledge of everything which will enable him to take control of his actions, and to reach a mental state which is properly attuned to the under-water environment. This is his best, and only, safeguard.

The structure of matter
All matter is composed of atoms with space between them. Everything, whether a solid, a liquid, or a gas, is formed of millions and millions of molecules, each of which is composed of one or more atoms. A typical example is the combination of two atoms of hydrogen with one of oxygen to form the molecule of water (28). The molecules of which matter is made up, are held together by a force, called molecular attraction, whose strength varies, dependent on the nature of the matter concerned, whether it is solid, liquid or gaseous.

In the case of a gas, the molecular attraction is low, therefore the molecules tend to move further apart from each other, and thus the weight of a gas is low. In liquids and solids on the other hand, they are held closer together, and thus the weights of these substances are greater.

There exists a relationship between molecular attraction and temperature so that the same substance can appear in different forms depending on whether it is hot or cold. A typical example is water, which becomes solid in the form of ice when cold, and becomes a gas in the form of steam when heated to a high temperature.

Specific weight
Everything has weight. Even the smallest part, such as a molecule of a gas, is pulled by the force of gravity to a lower level which, in our case, is towards the center of the earth. Obviously this attraction is different for every substance and is proportional to their different weights.

The weight of a substance per cubic centimeter of its volume, at normal temperature and pressure, is called its specific weight. For air it is .001, and that of fresh water is 1. A liter of air, therefore, weighs about 1 gram, while a liter of fresh water weighs 1 kilogram. The specific weight of sea water is 1.026, and that of human tissue is slightly over 1.

In this book we will use the following units of measurement (29):
1 *the meter* for distance,
2 *the kilogram* for weight,
3 *the second* for time,
4 *degrees centigrade* for temperature,
5 *atmospheres* or *bars* for pressure,
6 *degrees* for angles

Where necessary, imperial units will be shown in brackets as feet, pounds, degrees fahrenheit and pounds per square inch (14.7 equals 1 ATA).

29

30

Underwater, the concept of pressure recurs constantly, so that a knowledge of all problems related to pressure is essential to all who hope to dive, even in shallow water.

Pure water weighs one gram per cubic centimeter. Therefore a column of water 10 meters, or 1000 centimeters, deep produces on each square centimeter a weight of 1000 grams or one kilogram.

Air also has weight, and the weight of the average total depth of air in the atmosphere pressing on the surface of the earth at sea level is called one atmosphere, and in fact this is also equal to one kilogram per square centimeter. In barometric measurements the equivalent weight of a column of mercury (Hg) is used. This would be 760mm high and is expressed like this: 760 mmHg. From these measurements of pressure we obtain the following relationship.

One kilogram per square centimeter equals the weight of air at sea level, equals one atmosphere, equals ten meters of water, equals 760mmHg. Ambient water pressure is expressed in terms relative to the atmosphere and is known as atmospheres absolute (ATA). It is determined by adding the pressure of the atmosphere (1 AT) to the water pressure. Thus, at a depth of 10 meters the absolute pressure is: water pressure (1 At) + atmospheric pressure (1 AT) = 2 ATA.

Weight and pressure

The pressure transmitted through a fluid has the same force equally in all directions simultaneously, which is a condition that does not apply to solid substances (30). Pascal, after whom this principle is named, demonstrated it by using a pump with a bulbous container having holes all round. Forcing in the plunger caused equal jets of water to be projected from the container at all angles, and equal pressures to be shown on gauges.

The total atmospheric pressure acting on a man of average size at sea level is about 20,000 kilograms. This is calculated from the surface area of the average human body, which is about two square meters, multiplied by the average atmospheric pressure of one kilogram per

SOME BASIC PHYSICS

square centimeter. In the same way, a diver is subject to the pressure of the water, which acts on him from every direction and is distributed to all parts of his body with the same force (31). It is because this distribution is equal for all directions, and because human tissue is largely incompressible, that a diver is not crushed in deep water.

The human body has cavities which contain a mixture of gases. These cavities can be compressed until the gases in them maintain a balancing pressure equal to the external pressure applied to them. In cavities which cannot be compressed, the original pressure is maintained unchanged, and additional gas would be needed to counteract an increase in pressure.

Buoyancy

An object immersed in a liquid receives a buoyant thrust towards the surface equal to the weight of the volume of liquid which that body has displaced. This is Archimedes' Law; it decides whether the object will float on the surface or sink to the bottom.

If an object with a volume of one liter (1000cc) is immersed in water, it will displace an equal volume of water weighing one kilogram. The object will, therefore, receive a thrust towards the surface of one kilogram, and as a result, if it weighs less than one kilogram in air, it will float, whereas if it weighs more it will sink. If it weighs exactly one kilogram it will remain in hydrostatic balance.

A man in water is almost in hydrostatic balance. If he is breathing in and out as deeply as possible his volume will vary from about three liters more, to about five liters less, than his average. This means that in the first case he will receive a positive upward thrust (32), while in the second case he will tend to sink (33). In sea water, which weighs more than fresh water, the thrust is greater which makes it easier for a man to float.

This hydrostatic thrust is an impressive force: an airtight bag taken to the bottom of the sea and filled with air can support a tremendous weight. A bag containing air with a volume of 1000 liters, for example, can support a weight of one metric ton.

31

32

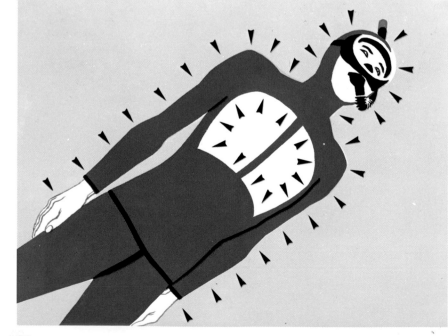

22

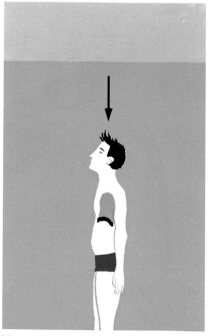

33

Pressure and volume in gases

Gases, as we have seen, are formed of molecules which have a natural tendency to move away from each other. If pressure is applied to the molecules of gas which, unlike a liquid, is compressible, the volume of the gas will be reduced. This leads to Boyle's Law of physics which states: at constant temperatures the volume of a given quantity of gas is inversely proportional to the pressure.

If we take as an example a cylinder containing a gas at a pressure of one atmosphere, it follows that doubling the pressure will reduce the volume to exactly half (34). Relating this example to sea level, where there is already an air pressure of one atmosphere, and immersing the object in water, we can see that at a depth of 10 meters (2 ATA) the volume will be reduced to a half, at 20 meters (3 ATA) to one third, at 30 meters (4 ATA) to one quarter and so on.

It is clear from this law that an increase in pressure always leads to a reduction in volume. In passing from a pressure of one atmosphere at the surface to a pressure of two atmospheres at a depth of 10 meters, the volume of the gas will be reduced to a half. The volume of air contained, for example, in an elastic balloon of 5 liters would become 2.5 liters: a real reduction of 2.5 liters. With an increase of one atmosphere from 30 meters (1.25 liters) to 40 meters (1 liter), that is from 4 to 5 atmospheres, the decrease in volume will be from one quarter to one fifth: a real change of only 0.25 liter.

The reverse of this process is of the utmost importance. If one fills a balloon with air in deep water and allows it to rise to the surface the volume will inevitably increase proportionally (35). The balloon may be elastic and capable of accepting this change—the human lungs on the contrary most definitely cannot do so, and this is a vital problem when diving with breathing apparatus.

The solubility of gases in liquids

Gases are soluble in liquids and there is an established law of physics which says that the quantity of a gas that can be dissolved in a liquid at a given tempera-

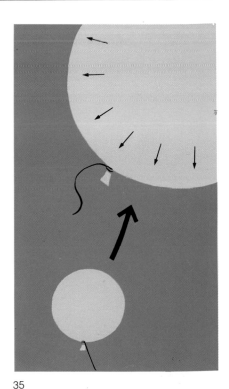

35

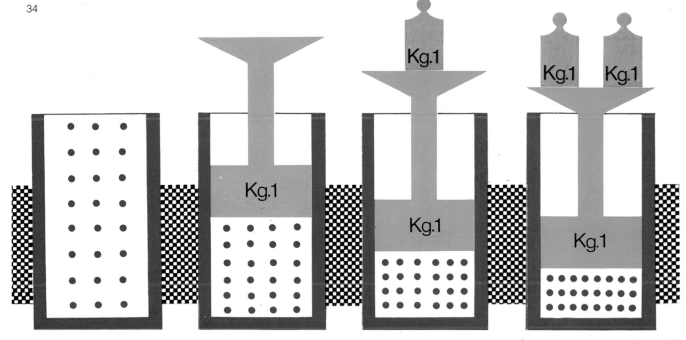

34

36

ture is proportional to the pressure of the gas at the surface of the liquid. There is a characteristic value for each individual gas and each individual type of liquid solvent.

If a gas is under pressure and in contact with the surface of a liquid, some of the molecules of the gas will be dissolved to the point where a state of equilibrium will be established between the molecules that are free and those that are dissolved—an equilibrium between the pressure of the compressed gas and the gas that is in solution (36). When this point is reached the solution is said to be saturated.

If the pressure is further increased,

additional molecules of the gas will pass into solution in proportion to any such increase in pressure, until a new state of equilibrium or saturation is reached. A reduction in the pressure of the dissolved gas will lead to a collapse of the state of equilibrium, and in order to restore it, the excess molecules in solution will be freed. A state of desaturation is thus set in motion which ends when a state of balance is once more reached. If the quantity of gas being freed from solution is very great, the phenomenon of bubble formation occurs. The molecules of the liquid are held together by molecular attraction, but when the force of the gas which is being freed from solution is

greater than the force of attraction of the liquid molecules, the gas molecules collect together into what we know as bubbles. This gives rise to the state called a gas embolism.

Gas mixtures

When the gas contained in a liquid consists of a mixture of different gases, they will dissolve independently of each other in proportion to the percentage which each represents in the mixture; that is to say, to its partial pressure.

The partial pressure of any one gas in a mixture is in direct proportion to the percentage that it represents. Therefore the total pressure of a mixture is the sum of the partial pressures of the various

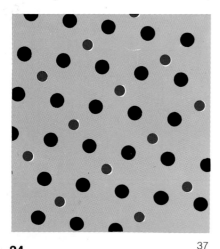

37

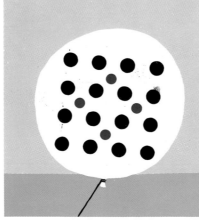

38

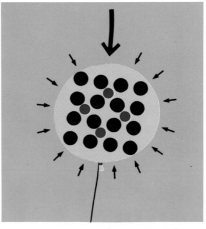

39

gases that it contains. The air we breathe, for example, is a mixture containing about 20 per cent oxygen and 80 per cent nitrogen, together with minute quantities of other gases (37). At sea level the partial pressure of the oxygen is about one fifth of an atmosphere, and that of nitrogen is about four-fifths (38). At a depth of ten meters of water the percentage composition of the air is unchanged, but by doubling the pressure on the mixture, i.e. to two atmospheres, the partial pressure of the two gases is also doubled, thus becoming about 0.4 of an atmosphere for oxygen and 1.6 atmospheres for nitrogen (39).

Temperature and pressure

An increase in temperature forces the molecules of a gas further apart, and consequently increases the volume, but if the volume cannot increase because the gas is restricted by a closed container, it causes a rise in pressure.

For example, if a full SCUBA cylinder is left in the sun the pressure will rise as it is warmed up by this external source of heat (41, 42). The temperature also can be changed by variations in the internal pressure. When cylinders are being charged, for instance, they heat up. If they are discharged quickly they can cool down to such an extent that ice can form on the valve (40).

This phenomenon also occurs in recompression chambers.

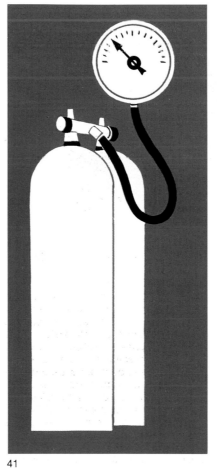

41

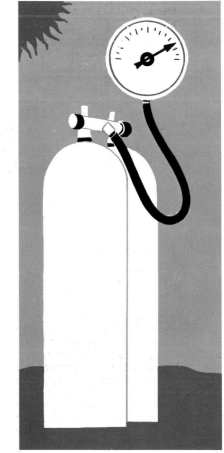

42

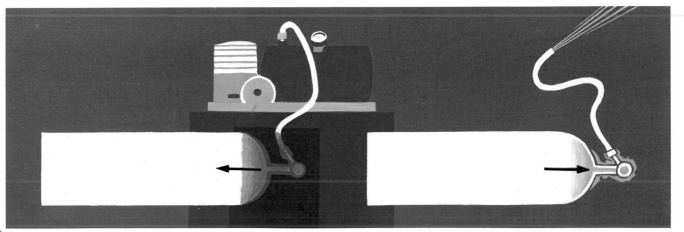

0

Some basic anatomy

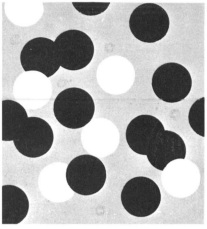

43

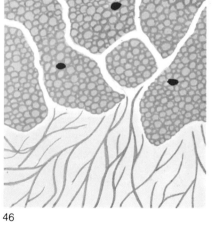

44

45

46

The human body

All forms of life are made up of cells. Some are unicellular while others, higher in the evolutionary scale, are made up of millions of these minute units. All have the common characteristic of needing oxygen and nourishment in order to produce, by a chemical process known as metabolism, the energy which is required for all living activity.

Almost 70 per cent of the human body consists of liquids and therefore, in accordance with the physical laws already discussed, they are able to dissolve those gases which come in contact with the blood through the surface membranes of the lungs, and which can thus be carried by it to all the tissues.

All the cells which make up living tissue are carried in intercellular substances which differ in consistency. In blood, for example, the cells (red and white corpuscles) are carried in a liquid intercellular substance (plasma) (43). On the other hand, in bone and cartilage, whose primary purpose is support, the intercellular substance is solid and rigid.

Nerve tissue is made up of star-shaped cells with extensions, whose functions are to carry information, and to direct and control the organism (44). Nerve cells have a low degree of resistance to a shortage of oxygen and nutriment, and they are affected more quickly than any of the others. If they are deprived of oxygen for a very few minutes many of them will die. Contrary to the life-cycle of almost all other types of cells, they do not multiply after the formation of the individual cell. In other words, damage to nerve tissue, even when it is limited to a few single cells, is irreversible.

Muscle tissue is formed of cells which have the power to contract, and consequently can do mechanical work (45). Some muscles are operated under voluntary control, others contract by an automatic mechanism. The first type includes the muscles with which we move the various parts of the body; the second type includes the heart.

Adipose tissue is made up of plump cells, full of fat, which serve as a nutritional reserve and as protection from the cold (46). They are slow, inactive and methodical in everything, but have a great capacity for accumulating.

The organs are made up of tissues put together for a specific purpose. A group of these, carrying out a common function, make up a system. As an example the cardiovascular system consists of the heart, the arteries, the veins and the capillaries. Another example is the skeletal system which is the frame which supports the whole body organism (47).

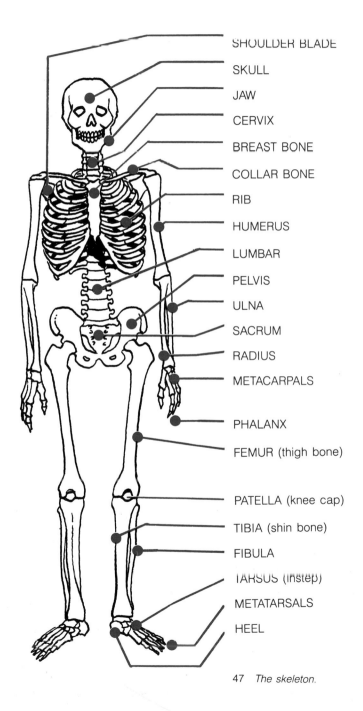

SHOULDER BLADE

SKULL

JAW

CERVIX

BREAST BONE

COLLAR BONE

RIB

HUMERUS

LUMBAR

PELVIS

ULNA

SACRUM

RADIUS

METACARPALS

PHALANX

FEMUR (thigh bone)

PATELLA (knee cap)

TIBIA (shin bone)

FIBULA

TARSUS (instep)

METATARSALS

HEEL

47   The skeleton.

The skeleton

The bones, which are the rigid organs that make up the skeleton, can be divided into those forming the head, the trunk and the limbs. They are of three types, which can described as long bones, short bones and flat bones.

The skin forms the external covering for the body, and its surface area averages two square meters (21½ sq. ft.).

The major units consist of the spine, which is built-up of 33 vertebrae, the skull, the ribs, the pelvis and the bones of the limbs. The first 7 vertebrae, known as cervicals, are those of the neck; the next 12 are the thoracics, which connect with the ribs, and these together with the breast bone form the rib cage. Higher up we find the shoulder blades and collar bones and the bones which form the upper limbs. The spine continues downwards to the lumbar region and the sacrum. The latter is connected to the hip bone and forms the pelvis, on which the lower limbs pivot.

The long bones have an internal cylindrical cavity which contains bone marrow. Of particular and practical interest for the diver, are the cavities found in the bony tissue of the skull known as the sinuses (frontal, maxillary, ethmoidal, sphenoidal) lined with mucous tissue, and which lead to the breathing channels of which they form part (48).

48

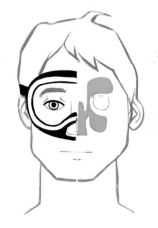

SOME BASIC ANATOMY

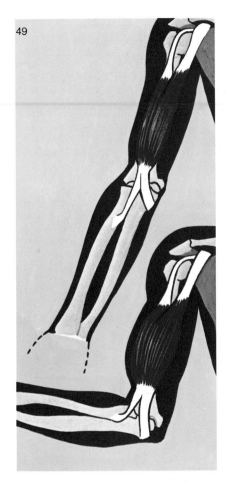

49

Muscles are attached to various parts of the skeleton, either directly or by means of tendons. Their cells have the ability to contract and thus vary the length of the muscle as a whole. The resulting displacement of the bone segments makes various movements possible (49).

Even breathing is produced by means of the muscles. The muscular diaphragm, and the muscles that act on the ribs, cause the necessary movement of the rib cage.

Temperature regulation

The skin, which is the outer covering of the body, is practically waterproof. Its main duties are that of protection, feeling, and temperature control. The human body has a normal average temperature of 37° C (98.4° F). The heat necessary to maintain this level comes from the natural functioning of the cells (metabolism) as a result of taking in nutrients and oxygen. In practice, the tissues produce energy in the form of heat as they are doing their normal work.

When the body temperature rises too high, the system spontaneously calls on the automatic method of temperature control, which is perspiration. Conversely, when the body becomes too cool an automatic mechanism causes involuntary muscular movements, such as shivering and trembling. When necessary the body can also produce a limited amount more heat by an increase in the rate of metabolism. These individuals with a thick layer of fat under the skin have an advantage as they have an inbuilt thermal insula-

tion, which enables them to endure the cold better.

The heart and lungs

We can consider the cardiovascular and breathing apparatus as being part of a single system because they both combine to supply the necessities for maintaining life and the ability to function to all the cells of the body. How they work is fundamental knowledge for the diver because of their essential roles in breathing, breath-holding, accidents and first aid.

Air contains approximately 20 percent of oxygen, nearly all the rest being nitrogen. Oxygen is the gas which is vital for the cells to absorb to live.

The breathing system (50) begins with a pipe, which starts from the mouth and nose, and continues with the pharynx, the larynx and the trachea. At this point the respiratory tube divides into two main branches, which continue to divide more and more frequently into ever finer tubes, to terminate in innumerable tiny cavities which are known as pulmonary alveoli (51). At the level of the larynx, immediately beneath the tongue, is the epiglottis which automatically closes off the tube leading to the lungs when one swallows food or liquids, and keeps it closed until these substances have passed into the oesophagus.

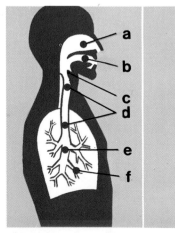

50
a *Nasal cavity*
b *Mouth*
c *Epiglottis*
d *Wind pipe*
e *Lungs*
f *Bronchial tubes*

51
1 *Lobe*
2 *Lung pockets (alveoli)*
3 *Pulmonary vein carrying oxygen*
4 *Pulmonary artery carrying carbon dioxide*
5 *Bronchial tube*

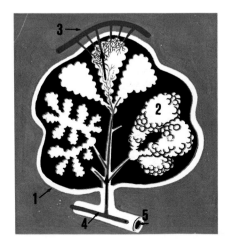

The cardiovascular system (52) consists of the heart, which acts both as a pressure and a suction pump, and the blood vessels in which the blood circulates. The left side of the heart (Red) receives blood from the lungs and forces it into a large tube, the aorta, from which smaller vessels branch off in all directions and lead to all parts of the body. Other vessels of ever decreasing size, leading off from these, join up with vessels which get larger and larger, and form the return circuit to the heart (Blue). The system of blood vessels, which starts at the aorta and returns to the heart after reaching all organs in the body, is called the primary circulation (B). That which goes from the heart to the lungs and returns to the heart is known as the secondary circulation (A).

We will now see how the system works (53). The lungs are contained within the rib cage and rest on a flat muscle, the diaphragm (–5), which separates the abdominal cavity from the thorax. The movements of the rib cage and the diaphragm produce the act of breathing which ventilates the lungs and maintains a constant level of oxygen and carbon dioxide in the pulmonary alveoli. A very thin membrane permeated with a fixed network of capillaries separates the air in the lungs from the blood, which is carried by the pulmonary circuit (A). The blood passes against the very thin walls of this membrane and is re-oxygenated through it and at the same time gives up carbon dioxide.

Thus the heart receives blood enriched with oxygen (–A to –1) and pumps it through the primary circulatory system to feed the cells of the various organs (–2 to –B); these take up oxygen and at the same time transfer to the blood carbon dioxide and other waste matter (–B). Entering the return circuit the blood, depleted of its oxygen and high in carbon dioxide, returns to the heart (–B to –3) from which it is pumped back to the lungs to be repurified (–4 to –A).

At various levels in the system there are nerve centers, which can signal a readjustment of the functioning of the breathing or the pumping as the situa-

52

53

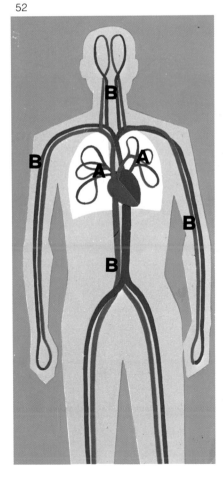

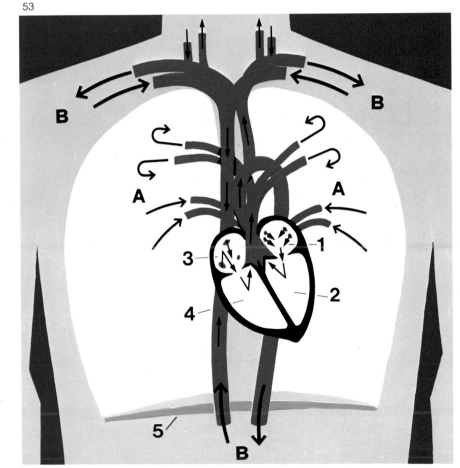

SOME BASIC ANATOMY

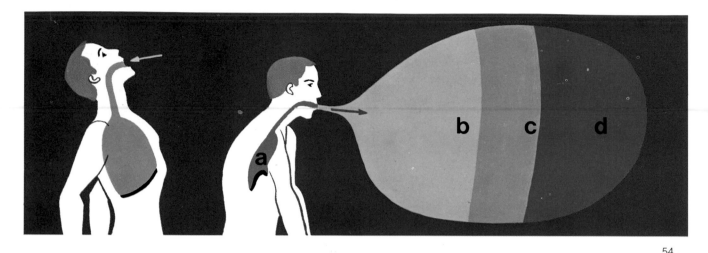

54

tion demands. During heavy manual work, for example, the cells carrying out the work need more oxygen. The rate of breathing increases, the heart accelerates, and the blood flows more quickly, to ensure that the muscles get the oxygen they need. The regulating mechanism, which controls the rate of breathing, is particularly sensitive to the level of carbon dioxide in the blood.

To understand clearly how it all works, the following facts should be noted:
● One normal act of breathing (the normal rate is 14 to 18 per minute) draws in about half a liter of air.
● The total quantity of air which it is possible to exhale, after one maximum inhalation is called the vital capacity ($54-b + c + d$). For a healthy man of 30, of average build, this is about 4–5 liters.
● The vital capacity can be thought of as consisting of a part which is normally breathed (c) called the tidal volume, an additional part extra which could be inhaled if needed (d), called the inspiratory reserve volume, and an additional part extra which could be exhaled if needed (b), called the expiratory reserve volume.
● After exhalation, i.e. after having emptied the lungs to the maximum extent, about one and a half liters of air will be left in the respiratory system and this is called the residual volume (a).
● The consumption of oxygen is about 20

liters/hour if the subject is at rest; at all other times it will be higher.
● The volume of blood in the body is about 6 liters. Life will be endangered if more than one and a half liters is lost.
● The heart beats about 70 times a minute and at each pulse it forces into the aorta 60–70cc of blood. This can go as high as 200cc during strenuous work.

The hearing system
The ear can be thought of as consisting of three parts:
1 The outer ear which is the ear flap together with the sound conducting channel;
2 The middle ear which is a cavity containing small bones which transmit the sound;
3 The inner ear, which is filled with an aqueous solution, and contains apparatus which can detect sounds and transmit them in the form of impulses to the brain. In this area there is also another structure which enables a person to sense his position, and thus to maintain his balance.

The outer ear is separated from the middle ear by a membrane called the ear drum (tympanum). The middle ear communicates with the pharynx, and then with the respiratory system, along a channel called the Eustachian tube. This channel is elongated, narrow, irregular, and has a tendency to become inflamed and blocked.

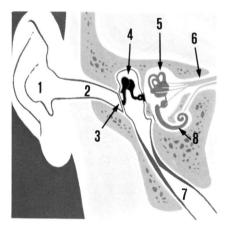

55

1 *Outer ear or ear-flap*
2 *Outer hearing channel*
3 *Eardrum (tympanum)*
4 *Anvil, hammer and stirrup bones*
5 *Semi-circular canals (balance)*
6 *Acoustic nerve and vestibular nerve*
7 *Eustachian tube*
8 *Cochlea (detection)*

Vision

The human eye is very similar to a camera (56). It comprises:

- The pupil (the diaphragm in the camera)
- The lens (the lens)
- The retina (the sensitized film).

From the retina the optic nerves transmit the image to the brain. To get a good photograph with a camera, it is essential that the subject should be accurately focused onto the film. In the same way, to get clear vision in the eyes, the image must be formed exactly on the retina.

The eyeball is filled with liquid and so there is no problem of changes in volume when diving. When the eye is in direct contact with water (57), on account of the differing angle of refraction of light in the denser medium, the image is formed in front of the retina and the picture will be out of focus and blurred, as in the case of an eye which is short-sighted.

On the other hand, if the diver is wearing a mask the situation is similar to someone looking into an aquarium through the glass (58): the view is sharp and clear because the refraction of the rays of light in passing from the water to the air brings the image nearer and enlarges it.

It is as well to be aware of this phenomenon. It would be disappointing to find, for example, that when a fish is caught and brought to the surface it turns out to be one-third smaller than expected! And it can be a major nuisance, particularly when snorkeling, to find that the exit hole in the cave, which looked big enough, was in fact much too narrow to pass through.

56

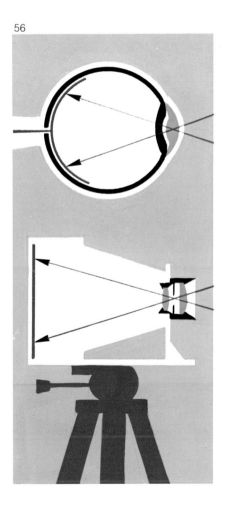

57

58

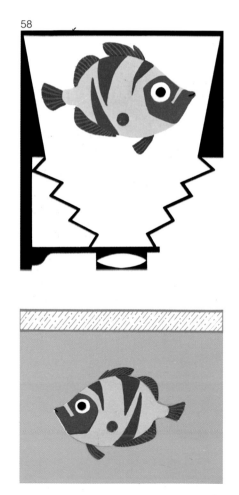

The human body underwater

59

Underwater temperature

A serious consideration for underwater divers is loss of body heat, because in water at a given temperature, the surface of the body loses twice as much heat as it does in air (59).

Reaction to cold, usually indicated by shivering, palpitations, a sense of constriction in the chest, chattering of the teeth and so on, differs considerably from person to person. A lowering of the general state of health, insufficient food, fatigue, or too much alcoholic drink all tend to make the human body more susceptible to the effects of cold.

The layer of fatty tissue under the skin is a useful insulation against the effects of cold, the amount of protection depending on its thickness.

Vagal inhibition

Vagal inhibition is a sudden and dangerous effect which is quite different from the gradual blocking of the breathing system which results from extended breath-holding.

It is characterized by a loss of consciousness and a sudden failure of the reflexes controlling the breathing and heart systems, which will be stopped permanently unless the victim is given immediate first aid. It can occur immediately on entering the water, or after any period of time.

There are many factors which can cause this condition, such as prolonged exposure to the sun and excessive sweating just before entering the water; diving straight into cold water instead of entering it slowly; repeated entries and exits from the water; intense emotional states.

Food for divers

Correct diet is particularly important from a safety point of view. It is helpful to develop, if possible, a layer of subcutaneous fat by eating fatty foods. The intake of sugar and vitamins can be increased with advantage during periods of frequent underwater activity. At busy times one should select foods with a high energy value and which are easy to digest. Diving should always be delayed until well after a meal, as the process of digestion places loads on many of the internal organs including the heart. In fact the loads on the central nervous system during digestion can bring on those nervous reflexes that are the cause of shock.

60

61 *Preparing to lift amphora.*

Hydro-shock is not always the result of entering the water immediately after a meal; however the danger does exist and one should, therefore, allow an adequate interval between eating a meal and diving. In cases where it is necessary to eat and continue diving immediately an easily digested form of sugar, such as dextrose, can be taken.

The work of the muscles in diving

In land based sports muscular work produces heat which causes a rise in body temperature (60). In diving, however, muscular activity generates less heat than the amount that is lost by the body to the water, even when working hard. Thus a comfortable body temperature cannot always be maintained. A diver must not try to restore the balance by extra physical effort. Fatigue and breathlessness would result and be ever more dangerous since they could lead to misjudgments and accidents. Physical effort must be carefully and intelligently controlled when diving, the aim being maximum efficiency with the greatest economy.

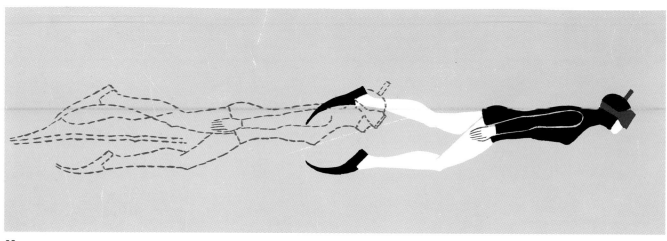

62

Underwater propulsion

With full breathing equipment, a diver normally uses only his legs for propulsion leaving the arms for controlling direction and for any other purposes (61). With no equipment at all, the breast stroke is best, but even this is less economical, less efficient and more tiring than using fins (62), and also needs the use of the arms as well as the legs (63). The other swimming strokes that are commonly used on the surface are no value under water.

The effects of water pressure

Underwater research workers have recently been subjected to pressures of more than 60 atmospheres, and animals to pressures in excess of 100 atmospheres, corresponding to depths of over 600 and 1000 meters respectively, without incurring any internal injury.

Tolerance to such pressures is possible due to the fact that the tissues and organs are made up basically of solid and liquid substances, which are not compressible, and that the functioning of the cells is not affected by high pressures of this order.

These experiments are even more amazing when one knows that even on the shallowest of dives it is essential that a careful balance is always maintained between the surrounding water pressure and that of the air in the body's cavities. This applies not only to dives using breathing apparatus but also to snorkeling.

When diving normally the balance in the major cavities, such as the lungs and the intestines and stomach, is maintained virtually automatically. Trouble often occurs however in the minor cavities such as the sinuses and ears.

63

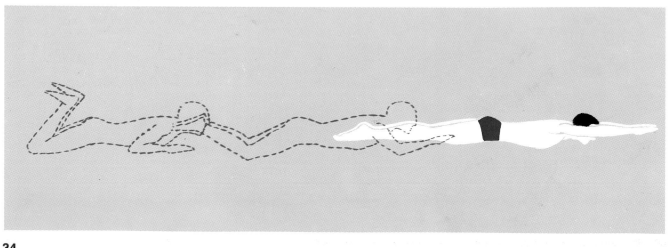

64

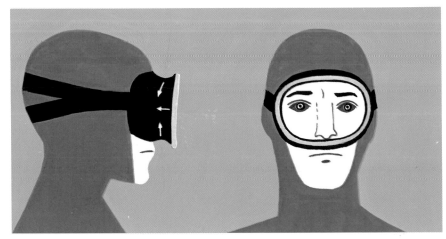

65

Pressure compensation in the mask and ear

The most frequently met example of unequal pressures occurs in the mask. The direct channel between the nose and the lungs becomes blocked by the soft palate, which rises by reflex action, and closes the passage between the pharynx and the nasal cavity. Therefore, when descending into deep water the external pressure and the pressure in the lungs rises, but this rise in pressure is not passed through to the mask. The pressure in the mask remains lower, and therefore has a sucking effect on the surrounding area of the face and is known as mask squeeze. This can act on the blood vessels in the eye and, if the difference is substantial, can cause them to expand to the point where some of the capillaries may burst (65). Such a hemorrhage is not usually serious, apart from causing bloodshot eyes which may last for ten days. To avoid this, all that is necessary is to blow some air deliberately into the mask via the nose, since this will force down the soft palate and equalize the pressure (64).

Unequal pressure also occurs fairly frequently in the middle ear and a pressure balance is rarely achieved automatically. The tortuous Eustachian tubes obstruct the adjustment of pressure and one must usually make a conscious effort to force a passage by using one of the techniques outlined on page 59. However, if the difficulty is due to a local infection it is not advisable to persist in trying to equalize the pressure. It is better to give up the dive.

The effect of pressure on the breathing system

The effect of the outside water pressure on the gas contained in the lungs, and the other air-filled cavities with which they are connected, is of the utmost importance and is different in the case of snorkel diving as compared to SCUBA diving.

In snorkel diving the lungs contain a fixed quantity of air at atmospheric pressure because the diver holds his breath. The water exerts pressure on this air by compressing the rib cage and the diaphragm. This causes a reduction in the volume of the air within the chest cavity until the air pressure becomes equal to the external water pressure. On rising to the surface the opposite occurs; the rib

66 *Snorkelers can reach these depths but they have to hold their breath.*

67

68

69

cage re-expands and the air returns to its original volume without any ill effects.

In the second case breathing can only continue if the lungs can receive and replace the air at a pressure very close to that exerted on the rib cage by the water outside. This can be demonstrated by going quite a short distance below the surface of the water and trying to breathe through a rigid tube leading to the air above. It is extremely tiring and you will have to give up quite quickly since the power of the muscles used in breathing is limited. They find it difficult to expand the rib cage even when the external pressure on the chest is only a little greater than the pressure of the air you are tying to breathe. It can be dan-

gerous to try and breathe air at atmospheric pressure like this when submerged and it should not be attempted.

When diving, the volume of air which the lungs hold will be less than the volume that this air would occupy on the surface, in accordance with Boyle's Law. For example, if at a depth of 60 meters (7 ATA) the lungs hold 6 liters of air, this quantity would expand to become 42 real, normal liters when transferred to the surface. It would be dangerous in the extreme to attempt to ascend from great depths when diving with SCUBA without releasing the surplus volume of air.

To avoid such a disastrous imbalance it is essential that a diver rising to the surface (67) should breathe continuously

(68). If he pauses, or worse, if he stops exhaling while the external pressure decreases, the volume of gas in the lungs will expand and may cause damage to the lung tissue (69).

Naturally the gases in the stomach and intestines are also affected by these same variations in pressure and volume.

Problems can be caused if, during the course of a dive, the volume of gas in the intestines should increase. On resurfacing one can experience unpleasant colic-like symptoms with painful distension of the abdomen. This can also affect the breathing or the heart and cause nausea, belching and flatulence, but these symptoms will disappear automatically in a short time.

70

71

72

The effects of pressure when snorkel diving

When living in the atmosphere conditions within the chest, which includes the secondary circulatory system of blood through the lungs, are continually being adjusted. The volume of blood in the circuit changes constantly to match the needs of the level of breathing, bouts of coughing or the body's muscular activity.

Changes in conditions when snorkel diving also cause automatic adjustment to be made. The pressure on the air in the lungs must conform to Boyle's Law. By the readjustment of its volume, it thus alters its pressure so as to balance the external pressure. The water pressure, however, is not in direct contact with the gas contained in the chest due to the way the body is constructed. So that, unless some other factor were to intervene, the pressure within the chest would tend to remain lower than that outside. When this happens it has an effect on the blood pressure, and this in turn leads to a balancing of the pressure in the following way.

The difference of pressure restricts the entry of blood into the left ventricle of the heart and boosts the return of the blood to the right auricle. This increases the volume of blood normally circulating in the pulmonary system, which helps to compress the gas in the lungs from within. This adds to the action of the increased water pressure which is operating from outside. The effect is to enable the snorkel diver to reestablish the pressure balance, and to reach depths which, under the normal laws affecting the pressures and volumes of gases, he could not otherwise attain (70, 71, 72).

In spite of recent studies, we do not yet have enough certain facts to establish the amount of extra blood which can accumulate in the lungs in this way, but it is in the order of a few hundred cc.

Fitness and safety

The basis of safety

In view of all that has been said about the environment, about physics and about the human body, it might be thought that only a superman could take up the sport of diving. On the contrary no special physique is required except a simple medical fitness check, similar to that used in other common sporting activities, together with a careful examination of the ears and their associated systems.

So a visit to the doctor for a routine check is the essential 'open sesame' to the underwater world, but this will not protect you against mishaps nor give you the right to act foolishly. Accidents in diving will occur with the same degree of probability, and with the same consequences, whether the individual is strong and athletic, or whether he is of less than average physique.

The preliminary medical examination is not able to reveal in advance certain reactions which diving may cause in particularly sensitive people. Such allergies usually show up in the form of nausea and headaches, which are not usually serious in themselves, but which can become extremely dangerous underwater. Because of this it is essential to carry out as much of the initial training as possible in a swimming pool where supervision is much easier, and later on, in company with another diver (73).

Sensitive conditions are usually rare and transitory, occurring in the early stages and disappearing as the diver becomes adapted. If this should not prove to be the case, it may be advisable to give up or to have a second and more detailed medical examination. After the training period, medical checks are again advisable before undertaking more serious diving.

38

73 *For safety divers always work in pairs.*

74 *Self-control is the basis of safe diving.*

Self control

An important aspect of fitness for diving is the diver's mental state, which can vary from time to time in a number of different ways. It is not likely to be constant because it depends on a combination of his knowledge, capability, determination and thoroughness, so that his attitude at any moment is governed by the effects of many variables. It will become stable only when his behavior in the water has become instinctive, and thus automatically reliable.

Other fundamental requirements for safe diving, which are often overlooked, are physical efficiency, which changes only over comparatively long periods, and physical condition, which can alter daily.

Physical efficiency depends on age, on fitness, on training and on the general state of health.

Physical condition can be affected by various, usually temporary, upsets including over-eating, excessive use of alcohol, stress and lack of adequate rest.

Both physical efficiency and physical condition are important because of the influence which they can have on how much the individual diver can do, and for their contribution to incidents or accidents.

The diver's emotional state is vital to his safety and must never be overlooked.

In an emergency no amount of the latest equipment, nor superior technique and ability, will be of any use unless they are backed up by self-control. Underwater it is essential to act and react quickly, coolly and with precision.

The basis of safe diving is self-discipline. It is not sufficient to limit the effects of an incident. Self-discipline must have the aim of avoiding the possibility of an accident ever happening. It should make the diver avoid ever becoming involved in a dangerous situation, forcing him to resist temptation, and into accepting that some sacrifices have to be made to be able to dive at all.

FITNESS AND SAFETY

Common sense

It can be dangerous to judge one's capabilities from a wrong basis. The amateur diver might not correctly assess the dangers of his own dives because he could be using information and statistics designed for champions, professionals, or, even worse, for very deep sea divers, forgetting that these experts are under medical control and are specially selected and trained (75). Their dives are programmed, and a support team of specialists is on hand to intervene immediately, when necessary, with the most up-to-date methods and equipment.

Amateur sport-divers should not forget that their greatest enemy is to be too enthusiastic. Often they do not realize that in many ways they are very exposed and unprotected. One sometimes hears of 'Sunday divers' taking part without any medical check-up, poorly prepared and equipped, untrained, without outside assistance. These are also the people who demand, in the few brief days that their free time allows, all that the sport can give, usually without stopping to ask what the cost might be. It is the enemies within themselves that are most to be feared: lack of discipline, lack of training, over-enthusiasm and inexperience.

Diving can be perfectly safe, but this depends above all on common sense. Instead of trying to compete with deeds which are really the province of only a few experts, a diver should prepare himself within his capabilities so that sport-diving becomes a relaxed recreation, no more dangerous than any other, with the advantage that he can put himself into a totally new existence, and yet be only a few feet under the surface of the sea. A diver can feel like a discoverer, an explorer and a conqueror, or he can watch and absorb the beauty and poetry of the undersea world.

Diving is a sport for everyone: the young, the old, men, and women. Young people in particular can benefit from diving because it will not overstrain the heart and blood circulation, but will greatly expand the lungs. A young person is also particularly well adapted to diving because he has rapid and positive reflexes which respond quickly to new situations.

Since great strength is not called for, women are physically on a par with men when diving. Their emotions are usually only external and they do not have the male aggressive instinct and tendency to exhibitionism which can be dangerous.

Recent medical studies have shown that elderly people can gain from diving with great benefit to the blood circulation in the legs, which tends to slow down with age. Furthermore, their natural thoughtfulness and instinct for self-preservation, and also their sense of responsibility, are more marked, and this automatically limits their actions to those that are within their capabilities and physical condition.

Most of all, common sense tells us never to dive alone. Our partner or diving buddy is the best safety device possible, and all our training is aimed at being able to give and receive help from him when it is needed.

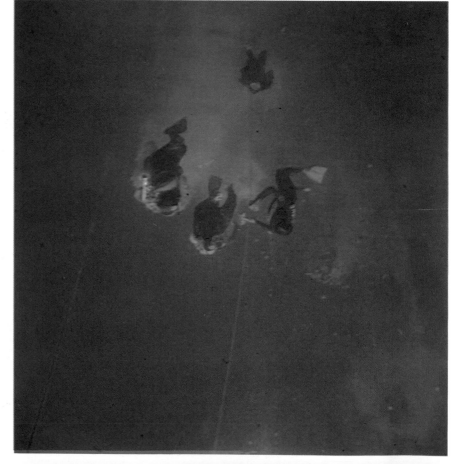

75 *Divers taking part in a snorkel record attempt.*

76 *Three different ways of entering the water.*

77 *Divers exchanging masks.*

PART

2

Snorkeling and Equipment

Equipment for snorkeling and SCUBA diving

79 Wet suits.

General
Equipment is defined as any tool, apparatus, or instrument which enables the diver to improve his performance or his capacity to adapt underwater. The diving suit, which is intended as a protection against cold, may or may not be used. For example, the snorkeler in the Caribbean will not need it, but the diver in the North Atlantic will certainly use one, along with various other accessories and instruments.

The equipment produced today is so comprehensive and wide ranging that even an expert finds it difficult to make a choice. One can start by considering utility and functional efficiency, but things immediately become complicated, because what appears to be essential to some divers is only regarded as averagely useful to others, or even quite unnecessary. The compass, for example, which is hardly mentioned in Italian diving manuals, is considered an essential by the

British in their cloudier waters, while the snorkel, which no Frenchman would be without, is barely used by the Germans.

There are no absolute rules or universal sets of recommended gear. Equipment which is ideal for use in warm tropic seas is not the same as that used in Arctic waters. Neither is it true that the specialist's gear will be better than the sportsman's outfit; it is simply different, being designed for different needs, and for use under different conditions. Nobody would normally use a long distance truck to commute to the office; it would be just as absurd to use a racing fin to go on an exploratory cruise underwater.

Diving suits
Some commercial divers use suits which stem from originals designed in 1837 as a result of the work of Augustus Siebe. It is the direct descendants of these that form the various types of diving suits which are today's wet-suits and dry-suits. The sports-diver of today uses mainly one type—the wet-suit made from foam neoprene.

The diving suit is called a wet-suit because a certain amount of water is allowed to seep in and fill any empty spaces between the diver's body and the suit. The water stays in the suit and is warmed by body heat, thus maintaining

80

81 *A full wet-suit with hood.*

a temperature which is more comfortable than that of the water outside. It is important that the suit is as close fitting as possible to restrict the space for water to a minimum. One should particularly avoid spaces under the armpits and along the back and sides of the body; these all form potential bellows that could suck in cold water from outside while the diver is working. The fewer routes there are for the water, the less will be the amount of water which will get in, and thus one will be less cold. For example, a jacket with an integral hood will be warmer than a jacket with separate hood.

There are many types of neoprene suits which can be adapted for different conditions, the first variation being in the thickness and weight of the material. A wet-suit is generally 3 to 6 millimeters thick (the latter for cold water), and can be single-skinned, double-skinned or lined with nylon fabric on one or both surfaces. The first two types are more flexible, but less easy to get into, while the opposite applies to the nylon-lined type.

The single-skin suit is spongy on one side and smooth on the other, the double-skin suit is smooth on both sides; the lined suit has fabric bonded to the surface.

To advise on a diving suit is a complicated problem, but it can be said that,

for someone who is going diving in temperate waters, a jacket or one-piece single-sided suit, 3–4mm thick is adequate. For dives in northern waters a 5–6mm thick suit, boots and gloves will be necessary.

45

EQUIPMENT FOR SNORKELING AND SCUBA DIVING

Weighting and the buoyancy compensator

If a diver increases his equipment, his weight adjustment in relation to the water will alter. He must compensate for these variations so that he maintains a state of neutral buoyancy.

As an example, a diver wearing a wet-suit and equipped with breathing apparatus, but with no weights will, on entering the water, have a positive buoyancy of 5 to 15 kilograms.

To add to the complications a wet-suit has a positive buoyancy of a few kilograms near the surface, but in deep water it is almost neutral, as the cells of gas which it contains will become reduced in volume on account of the surrounding pressure. For example, a wet-suit that has a positive buoyancy of 4 kilograms at the surface, will have little more than one kilogram at 30 meters.

Weight adjustment with lead weights on a belt (82) to obtain perfect equilibrium is thus more theoretical than real, and it also varies according to the length of the dive on account of the weight of compressed air that has been used. 1.3 kilograms of lead must be added for every cubic meter of air which is used up. The only effective way of solving the problem is to use a buoyancy compensator, or which there are various types. They can be inflated by several means and allow the diver to adjust his buoyancy at any time so that he can reach equilibrium at any depth (83). In Britain this is known as the Adjustable Buoyancy Life Jacket (ABLJ).

The dual role of the buoyancy jacket is important to divers' safety. First of all it avoids fatigue, since the diver can always attain neutral buoyancy, and thus avoid over-exertion. Secondly it will allow him to reach the surface in an emergency and support him while he is there, or even give similar assistance in rescuing a companion diver. Some models even incorporate a facility which allows the diver to breathe air from the jacket should his regulator fail. Ideal features are that it should be easy to put on; should not interfere with the use of other equipment (weight belt, regulator, taps); it should be

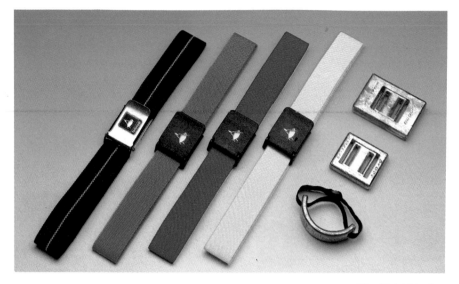

82 *Weight belts.*

83 *Buoyancy compensator.*

possible to inflate it by alternative methods; and finally, it must be designed so that it will keep the wearer's head above the surface of the water.

Fins

It is not easy to say definitely what makes a good fin. The difficulty becomes greater if judgment is based on the commercial success of the different types. For mysterious reasons, some of the least efficient, least comfortable and least economical are among those most widely used.

Some of the qualities which should be included among those of an acceptable fin are:

- The blade angled at 20°–30° in relation to the foot, so that it is more nearly parallel to the axis of the leg, rather than the foot.
- The foot pocket, made from soft rubber, the blade and the thicker part from hard rubber.
- The plane of thrust should be symmetrical, and thus they should be interchangeable between feet.
- The toes should be free.

84 *Fins.*

85

Fins must not be too tight, particularly over the instep, as this may restrict the circulation and cause numbness. Nor should they be too large as they will tend to chafe and rub the skin causing abrasions. Try them on over your wet-suit boots when buying to ensure a comfortable fit.

86 *Snorkels.*

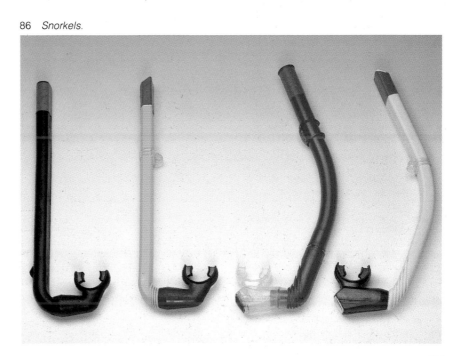

The breathing tube (snorkel)

The tube used for breathing on the surface with the face underwater, is the basic tool of the snorkel diver (86). It is also useful to the SCUBA diver, especially on the surface in rough seas after the air in the cylinder is exhausted. It is the simplest piece of equipment but is not the most standardized as it comes in many styles.

A soft tube is better than a rigid one, a fairly large diameter rather than a narrow one (20 millimeters is about right), and a smooth tube is better than a corrugated one. Its usefulness for underwater work is beyond question and it is preferred by those for whom the simplest things are the best.

87 *Single glass mask.*

88 *Twin lens masks.*

The mask

In shape and color the choice of a mask can be a matter of personal taste, but it should have the following features (87, 88, 89):

● maximum field of view;
● a perfect seal on the face;
● provision for blowing one's nose to compensate for pressure;
● leave the mouth uncovered;
● the internal volume should be the minimum possible;
● fitted with safety glass;
● if it has separate eyepieces they should be optically identical (88)

When trying it on make sure that it does not cause wrinkles at the base of the nose and at the hair line; these would form points of access for water. Put it onto your face without using the strap and breathe in gently through the nose. It should stay in place by suction. If a mask stays in place by itself for about fifteen seconds it is a good fit; if it does not, try another model.

The depth gauge

The depth gauge is a pressure gauge which is calibrated in depths (90). Cheaper models use an air column to register the pressure, and if constructed in accordance with the principles of Boyle's Law will indicate moderate depths accurately, but are not suitable for greater depths. More expensive types give a more reliable reading in both cases. A beginner will find the air type quite adequate for the relatively shallow dives that he should concentrate on initially.

89

90 *Depth gauges.*

The underwater gun

The basic characteristics are (91, 92):
- simplicity of construction because the fewer parts there are the less likely it is to jam;
- accuracy;
- easy to reload;
- good balance and comfortable stock;
- powerful penetration by the harpoon;
- simple to maintain;
- reasonable running costs.

The absence from this list of the words 'power' and 'long range' will be noted.

The reason is very simple; underwater it is a waste of time to fire at anything more than four meters from the point of the harpoon. Beyond this recommended maximum range the problems of accurate aiming, and the moment to pull the trigger, are too complicated.

Apart from the spring operated type, there are two other possible choices; operation by compressed air or by elastic. Anyone who is going to take up hunting should appreciate that you do not go looking for small fish with the same armament that you would need for larger prey.

It is, perhaps, worth mentioning the 'power-head', which is probably the best, if not the only effective defensive weapon available. Developed in Australia as a defense against sharks it consists of a cartridge which is enclosed in a waterproof container and fixed to the point of the harpoon. Fired from the normal underwater gun, on impact with the prey a percussion cap fires the cartridge, and the shock waves are usually sufficient to kill instantly.

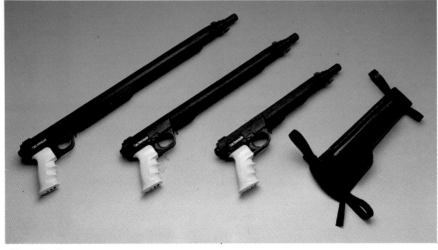

91 92 *Guns.*

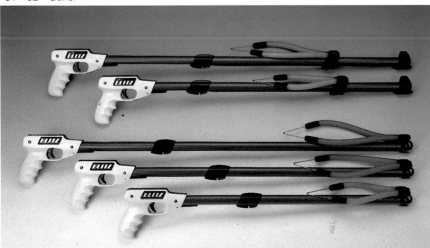

The watch

Waterproof watches are available today in a wide variety of styles. It is not necessary to spend a fortune on a watch, but it is not advisable to try and be too economical. The seals should be checked at least every two years. The revolving bezel is essential on a diver's watch and is set at the start of the dive so that one can always tell how long the dive has lasted (93).

93 *A diver's watch with bezel.*

EQUIPMENT FOR SNORKELING AND SCUBA DIVING

The marker buoy

This is an air filled buoy whose object is to indicate the presence of divers below (94). It must be strong and resistant to abrasion and puncturing. It can be rigid or inflatable and large enough to support a flag which is visible from a distance. The colors of the flag, which is fixed to the top of the buoy, are a matter of some controversy: the international rules of navigation require blue and white but in the US a red flag with a white line is used.

The knife

There are occasions when a knife can save one's life. Always useful, and at times indispensable, it will be used during its lifetime for purposes which its maker would never have dreamed of.

It is the most useful general purpose tool and one should look for a knife which has a majority of these characteristics (95):

- stainless steel blade, sharp, strong and pointed;
- a comfortable and firm handle;
- a sheath which covers the blade completely, with an opening to let the water out, and a secure fastening which at the same time will not create difficulty when you wish to draw it.

Self-contained underwater breathing apparatus (SCUBA)

Rouquayrol-Denayrouze in 1860, Le Prieur in 1926, Commeinhes and Cousteau-Gagnan in 1943, it seems appropriate that the history of automatic pressure regulation and SCUBA should have been written in French.

The basic purpose of the regulator is to transform the air from the cylinder, where it is at high pressure, to the mouthpiece at a low pressure to conform with normal breathing at any depth; that is to say, at the same pressure which exists in the diver's lungs. This adjustment is essential bearing in mind what was said about the inability of the chest muscles to expand the lungs when the outside pressure is higher than that inside.

94 *Signal floats.*

95 *Knives.*

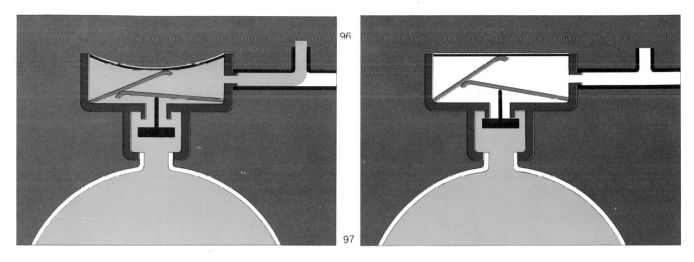

96

97

The basic regulator can be thought of as being like a cup covered with a rubber membrane. As the diver inhales he causes a suction within the cup. This suction draws the membrane inwards and this opens the valve via a lever connected to it. The air in the cylinder is released and can be breathed (96). Breathing out returns the membrane to its normal position, causing the valve to close and stay closed until the next breath is taken (97).

There are two main groups of regulators; the single-stage with two hoses (98) connecting the regulator to the mouthpiece, and the two-stage which has only one hose connecting the two stages (99). In the single-stage type the cylinder pressure is reduced to ambient pressure in only one step. In the two-stage type, however, it is reduced in two steps; in the first stage the pressure is 8–10 atmospheres more than the ambient pressure and the pressure in the mouthpiece. In the second stage the pressure is reduced still further to balance the ambient pressure.

This is beyond question the most vital piece of equipment for a diver to have and only the best is good enough.

A regulator must have the following features:

- be exactly able to regulate the supply according to the diver's demands and without waste;
- low resistance to the breathing action of the lungs at all depths, both on inhaling and exhaling;
- robust construction of the body and the tubes;
- easy clearance of water from the regulator.

As far as the last feature is concerned a beginner should note that the two-stage type empties itself much more

98 *Single-stage regulator.*

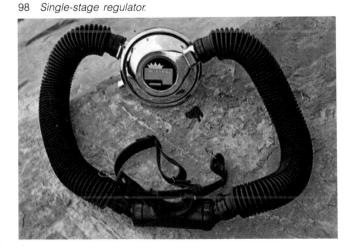

99 *Two-stage regulator.*

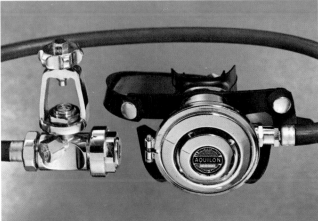

EQUIPMENT FOR SNORKELING AND SCUBA DIVING

easily, quickly and safely, without requiring the movements or the contortions which are sometimes necessary with the single-stage type. Another point is that the two-stage type is much more robust, and also the diver can operate it by hand to release air from the cylinder without using the lungs. In cases of severe breathlessness or other emergency it is therefore possible to continue to breathe by mechanical means.

Tanks and tank valves

With cylinders or tanks today the worldwide trend is away from steel and towards an aluminum alloy, which can give a high degree of proof against corrosion. In the fight against corrosion experiments are also going on with other materials, but so far they have not yet shown any practical advantages over the traditional steel cylinders, which can give good results with the special anti-rust treatments which many industries use today.

Cylinders can be of various capacities, and breathing apparatus is designed for use with one or more cylinders (102, 103), or built into a back-pack. We will leave the three cylinder models to the

100   *Tank valves.*

101   *Valve and reserve fittings.*

experts, but note that extra long cylinders are likely to be difficult to manage for small divers.

The valves or taps are not so very different in principle from those of a normal household water tap. Air at a high pressure comes out of one and water at a much lower pressure out of the other. Each is designed and made in such a way that it is not necessary to use force to close it. To do so will damage it.

Some taps may have a built-in reserve device which allows the main supply to drop to 25%-30% of the original pressure of the charge, after which it automatically cuts off. The diver will notice when this moment approaches because he will have a slight difficulty in breathing, which will increase gradually and steadily. He will therefore have plenty of time, before breathing becomes impossible, to operate the lever or wheel which

102   103   *Single- and twin-cylinder tanks.*

opens the reserve supply.

In some valves the reserve apparatus is semi-automatic, and can only be opened when the pressure drops to that of the reserve supply. This is useful because if it gets a knock it cannot open too soon, and thus one avoids the fear of finding that, at the moment when you need it, the reserve supply has been accidentally used up already.

Most regulators and some valves have provision for connecting a submersible pressure gauge. This gives you another way of checking your reserve of air, but of course you must remember to look at it. However, the visual gauge has the advantage that one can calculate at any moment from the pressure indicated, the volume of air still available. Without such a fitting one can only measure the pressure before starting a dive by using a suitable separate pressure gauge (104).

The decompression meter

It is necessary here to mention the decompression meter even though to begin with it is better to use only a watch, a depth gauge and a decompression table.

The use of the watch and depth gauge together with the tables, which can be obtained printed on plastic sheets, will enable the beginner to learn their use automatically. It is important to practice such routines because it is more difficult under water to make even the simplest of calculations. Training in this may prove to be vital some day. It is important also to plan any decompression stops before entering the water, and it is highly recommended that one avoids dives which requires stage decompression.

The decompression meter (105) is an instrument which displays on a dial by means of a needle the stage at which nitrogen starts to be passed into solution within the tissues during the duration of a dive. This occurs when the pressure is greater than that of the gas in solution. It also indicates during resurfacing, the point when the outside pressure becomes less and the gas starts to be liberated from the tissues.

It is useful because, among other things, it takes account of every variation of depth and shows a continuous summary: a situation which could not be otherwise known except by calculation and the use of a watch and depth gauge.

The dive computer

Dive computers have been introduced in recent years. The dive computer provides the diver with the following information: current depth, maximum depth, total bottom time, remaining time to ascend to the surface within the safety curve and all information on decompression. It will also calculate the number of dives. Some more elaborate computers can be used for high altitude diving up to 4000 meters. The computer works at every depth. The usefulness and accuracy of the dive computer is still being debated. The simpler models should suffice for the recreational diver.

104 *Underwater contents gauge.*

105 *Decompression meter.*

106 *Dive computer.*

The underwater light

Used in daylight at great depths or where the sunlight is unable to penetrate, and everywhere at night, it helps to restore natural color to everything falling into its beam.

It must:

- be waterproof;
- have approximately neutral buoyancy;
- have a powerful light;
- have a well focused beam;
- be operated by one hand;
- be able to withstand the pressure.

107 *Waterproof lights for underwater use.*

Maintenance of the equipment

Metals and salt water have never got on well together; neither does fine sand agree with delicate apparatus. It is therefore essential to rinse everything in fresh water, often and carefully. At the sea bottom the breathing equipment should never remain for long in a muddy area; mud is abrasive.

Use a rubber cap to seal the regulator inlet when it is not in use. The cap should be removed when assembling the equipment and replaced when it is dismantled, making sure that it is dry. If there are any doubts that fresh water may have leaked into the regulator, reassemble it and blow air through it several times; the air which passes through will be enough to expel the water. If salt water has been allowed to enter, then the regulator may need to be examined inside.

It should always be remembered that everything used in sea water becomes encrusted with salt; therefore after diving wash everything in plenty of fresh water. For rubber it is sunlight that causes the damage, so it should be kept in the shade. If the equipment will be out of use for a period, dust the rubber parts well with talc or french chalk, and grease the metal parts (preferably with a silicone grease).

The tanks need checking internally for rust or leaks. There are regulations in all countries which require them to be sent for hydrostatic testing after a certain period.

Some twin-sets have two inlets allowing two separate regulators to be fitted. Alternatively, some regulators are fitted with two second stages or mouthpieces. Dual types are advisable if the divers are going down to any great depth, because the one in use might become blocked, or perhaps it might be necessary to provide air for a colleague in difficulty. Even though you are not yet an expert you should consider selecting this type of dual valve breathing apparatus from the start.

108 *Twin-hose, single-stage regulator.*

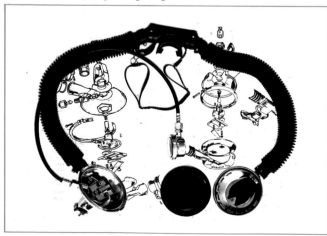

109 *Single-hose, two-stage regulator.*

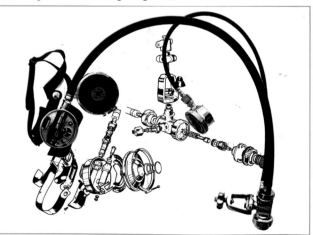

110 *A racing mono-fin which is flipped like a fish's tail.*

Problems in snorkel diving

General

Diving in general is subject to rules and limitations which one must know and observe to avoid accidents, and this is especially so in snorkel-diving, which is in many ways quite different from diving with an aqualung (SCUBA).

A diver who has not taken the trouble to prepare himself will be particularly affected by conditions in snorkel diving. Nervousness may cause him to interrupt his dive prematurely and this will be due to poor mental preparation and not because of any physical necessity.

Indeed a properly prepared novice diver, who is trained and mentally relaxed, can expect to be capable of holding his breath for the following periods:

● 15—30 seconds after breathing out;
● 30—45 seconds after a normal breath;
● 1 minute—1 minute 30 seconds after taking a deep breath;
● 1 minute 30 seconds—2 minutes 30 seconds after brief hyperventilation (see later) and the greatest possible deep breath.

From this it can be seen that deep inhalation and hyperventilation (which is explained shortly) are of help in snorkel-diving, where performance can be improved by practice, but they can cause a serious situation if they need to be used in an emergency and without proper training.

The effects of prolonged breath holding

During a prolonged dive the exchange of gases can continue only for a limited time because the lung pockets gradually collect an increasing amount of carbon dioxide (black dots in fig. 111) while the oxygen (red dots) decreases. This leads to the gas content of the blood being also affected and it becomes unable to carry out its task, and this acts first on the nerves controlling breathing. It leads to a state of panic called 'suffocation' which is combined with a contraction of the ribs and the diaphragm. If the diver cannot prevent this, that is by resuming breathing, at a certain point he will lose consciousness with his mouth closed. He will be unable to breathe owing to a paralysis of the breathing nerves. This symptom of prolonged breath holding can arise either from an excess of carbon dioxide tension, or from a shortage of oxygen (hypaxia), or by a combination of both factors.

The possibility of prolonging a dive depends on several factors. We have mentioned deep breathing and hyperventilation but it would also be affected by the greater rate of heat loss in water and the using up of muscular energy. Note that the loss of heat is of the greatest importance. Unnecessary exertion, when the diver's skills and techniques are imperfect, is also a factor.

Breath holding underwater

There is one effect of the underwater conditions which is actually favorable to the human body—the so called 'Diving Reflex'. This can be demonstrated by putting one's head under water (112) when it can be shown that there is a slowing of the heart beats of the order of 30—40 per cent. Another way of putting it is that in deep water the pressure of the gas mixture in the lungs is raised by external pressure, as has already been explained. Consequently when the percentage of oxygen in the blood has fallen to an inadequate level, the partial pressure of the oxygen in the mixed gas in the lungs may be too low, on account of the depth, to enable it to re-oxygenate the blood and the tissues.

In a case of breathing paralysis caused by over-prolonged breath holding, the danger is not too serious provided the victim can be brought back into the open

111

air. It is only the respiratory system which is stopped and he can be revived without difficulty. In a case where the diver cannot be brought to the surface rapidly, the chances of recovery will be slight, and none at all if the delay is of the order of 10 minutes.

Though the apparently adequate pressure of oxygen when deep diving seems to preclude loss of consciousness this can, even so, be caused by a scarcity of the gas. This occurs when prolonged hyperventilation has lowered the level of carbon dioxide. This condition is reached when one has been breathing more deeply and at a greater rate than normal. It used to be called hyper-oxygenation but is now more correctly termed hypocapnia (reduced carbon dioxide tension).

Hyperventilation
To improve the length of dives, it is possible to hyperventilate the lungs which means breathing more deeply or more frequently than normal, or both, for a period before entering the water. It is most effective if the lungs are deflated to the greatest possible extent, thus expelling air to the maximum, rather than the other way about, i.e. after a deep inhalation. The total efficiency of the method depends on the number of breathing cycles made per minute. If this is done thoroughly for some time it slightly raises the oxygen level, but can reduce to a much greater extent the level of carbon dioxide.

Prolonged hyperventilation is only permissible for someone who has undergone training. Otherwise it can cause a tingling sensation, dizziness and muscular spasms which are the danger signals of the onset of those contractions of the ribs and of the diaphragm which indicate the limits of breath holding and lead to breathing paralysis. This technique is not recommended for beginners.

112 *Testing the 'diving reflex'.*

The sinuses and the middle ear

The pressure in the chest cavity is maintained constantly in balance with the pressure outside and normally this balance adjusts itself automatically via the channels that lead to the nasal sinuses. However, it rarely passes without help through those connected with the middle ear, known as the Eustachian tubes.

It is only when there is local inflammation, that equalizing the pressure in the sinuses causes any difficulty, because the channels concerned are short and of adequate size. If, however, the tubes are blocked and the cavity concerned is at a lower pressure, a diver can suffer intense pain. In such a case it is advisable to stop diving until the inflammation subsides. If the pain persists when on the surface, it would be advisable to see a doctor.

The Eustachian tubes which lead to the middle ear are long and narrow and are partially blocked in the middle. Because of this, and particularly in the case of any inflammation, very few people can achieve a balance automatically.

In the sinus cavities a fairly considerable lowering of pressure can be tolerated, but the middle ear contains the thin membrane called the eardrum which has limited stretch (113). When the pressure outside the eardrum exceeds the internal pressure the membrane is bent inwards (114), causing pain, and if the pressure difference is too great it can burst (115). In such a case the shock of the sudden violent inrush of cold water can affect the delicate mechanism of the inner ear. Apart from the piercing pain there will be a sensation of giddiness and loss of orientation which, for someone in a snorkel dive, can be very serious. A diver with breathing apparatus, on the other hand, can expect the effect to wear off while he returns to the surface, and so for him it is less likely to be disastrous.

On rare occasions it can happen that the pressure in the cavity cannot automatically drop while resurfacing because of internal inflammation or an obstruction. If this should happen the tympanum can burst outwards (116). In such a case there is no violent inrush of cold water, but there will be an explosive release of air and a giddy sensation.

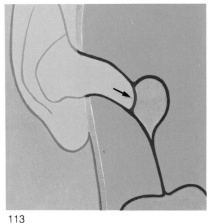

113

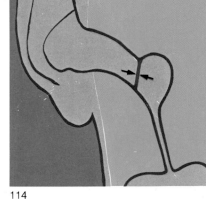

114

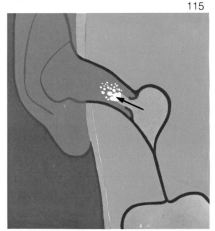

115

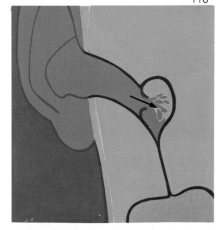

116

'Clearing' the ears

In the rare cases when the pressure in the sinuses does not equalize itself spontaneously, it is better to give up diving. With the middle ear, on the other hand, nearly everyone will have difficulty to a greater or lesser extent, and a state of balance can only be obtained by using one of the following techniques.

The exercises to be done are of two types; by movement (not very efficient) which one carries out with the nose open, and by pressure (very effective) which is done with the nose closed.

The movement exercise consists of contracting the back of the mouth, chewing motions or swallowing and is thus very easy to do (117, 118).

There are two pressure exercises and the more commonly used is known as the Valsalva (119). This is done by pinching the nose and trying to breathe out. The air enclosed in the lungs cannot escape and thus its pressure increases. It works best following a deep breath.

The Valsalva, however, is not an exercise which can be recommended because it causes variations in the blood circulation. It is preferable to use the Marcante-Odaglia method (120) which only affects the pharynx (throat). It does not cause any alteration in the circulation and is also the most efficient method.

The tongue is pressed against the palate and arched at its root so that it rises to close off the nose passages isolating them from the mouth and the lungs. With the nose closed, the tongue thus swells up acting as a pump, and raises the pressure of the air trapped in the pharynx. At the same time it presses against the local muscles, which pull on the walls of the Eustachian tubes, causing a powerful expansion.

The Marcante-Odaglia method also works just as well if done while exhaling. Unlike the Valsalva, communication between the pharynx and the lungs is closed during this exercise, and thus the possibility of transferring to the lungs the increase of pressure caused by the descent will be avoided.

During the progress of a dive it is recommended that the ears are 'cleared' frequently, since otherwise the pressure in the ear will exert a pumping force on the inner part of the Eustachian tube, thus making compensation more difficult, if not impossible. 'Clearing' is not intended to remove pain caused by an ear drum which is already bent inwards, but to prevent it from happening in the first place.

117

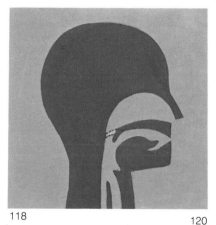

118

119

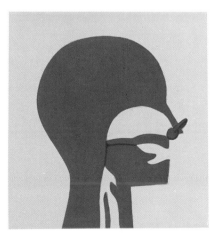

120

Swimming techniques without equipment

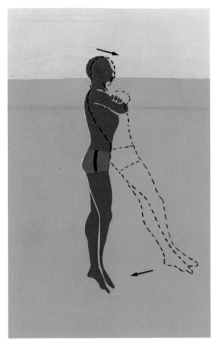

121

122

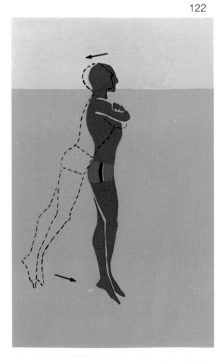

Confidence and ability

A diver who behaves rationally and efficiently in a smooth and quiet manner shows that he is 'at home' in the water. Therefore the true protection against drowning is not so much swimming ability but rather the swimmer's confidence in being able to master the conditions. It is not difficult to get results when wearing fins, mask and SCUBA, but it is not nearly so easy to manage without the aid of equipment, that is when swimming with the body free. Therefore a man's confidence when swimming unaided is the true basis for assessing his capability underwater.

To lack confidence in the water is a disadvantage. This shows in a man's breathing which becomes rapid and shallow and affects his buoyancy. This is the reason for the poor capacity and endurance of the beginner.

In learning to swim the techniques to be mastered include, not only the actual movements but also breathing, relaxation of the body and the smooth combination of all these things. So the first lesson is to learn to move slowly and smoothly and with the correct breathing, and nothing more should be attempted until this routine is perfect.

Every movement of the limbs which moves or supports the body in the water consists of two distinct phases. The first is called *the stroke* and is active; the other, which returns the limb to the position from which it can start the next stroke, is passive and is called the *recovery*.

Recovery movements underwater, especially those of the legs in the breast stroke, must be carried out accurately and smoothly. If this is not done the movement will tend to counter the work done by the power stroke.

The movements in any exercise should have a definite rhythm and coordination. The crawl is a typical example, where it is essential to coordinate breathing with the movements of the arms and legs.

Buoyancy of a free swimmer

In normal circumstances a man's body will float. To prove this all that is necessary is to set oneself upright in the water, breathe in and remain perfectly still (123). Average specific gravity varies from person to person, but as a general rule it is found that in fresh water a man will float with his nose at water level, whereas in salt water the level will be at his chin. A person with a high specific gravity will float rather lower, and one with a low specific gravity will float higher.

In salt water a buoyant body will not normally remain vertical because the hydrostatic thrust will turn him horizontal (121, 122). To stay in a vertical position all that one needs to do is to bend one's head and neck towards the direction in which the feet are starting to float up.

123 *Demonstrating the body's specific gravity.*

Arm movements

To turn forwards and somersault the arms are held straight out and the body is bent to an angle of 90°. They are also held straight as a part of the recovery and of the stroke. In the former the arms are moved backwards as much as possible with the hands edge on to the water (125). In the stroke the arms, which are first stretched backwards and slightly apart, are then brought forward, held straight and with the palms of the hands pressing on the water (126).

To practice this, hold yourself steady with the body vertical in the water. Make a breast stroke movement with the legs and give a strong downwards stroke with the hands, which will push you as high out of the water as possible. Remain as though standing to attention and hold this position while the body sinks. When you have gone as deep as possible bend 90° at the waist and use the arms as described above to continue turning forward in the vertical plane. During this movement draw the thighs up against

the chest and the legs against the thighs (124). In this compact position go on turning forwards by thrusting upwards with the palms of the hands.

If it does not work correctly it means that either the stroke is not being made properly or the arms, at the end of the recovery movement, have not reached back far enough. If the body does not remain in the vertical plane during the turn it means, either that the arms are being used unevenly, or that one has been used more powerfully than the other, or has not been fully extended, or the position of one hand in relation to the forearm is wrong. To work properly in water the hands must always be in line with the forearm with the fingers stretched out and together.

124   *A rolling surface dive.*

125

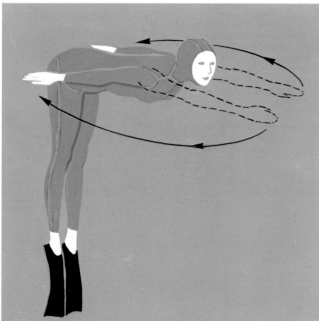

126

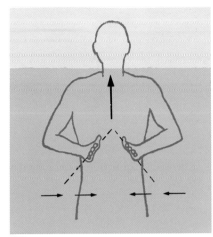

127

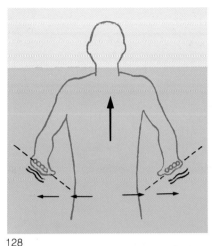

128

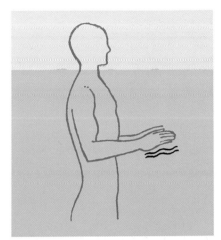

129

Supporting oneself on the surface

To support oneself on the surface the movements used are mainly the leg movements of the breast stroke with additional help from the hands moving in opposite directions to each other.

The arms are bent at the elbow at 90° and approach (127) and move away (128) from each other while remaining in a horizontal plane. At the same time the palms of the hands are angled to the horizontal, switching from one angle to the other in sympathy with the arm movements, so that they press down on the water (129). The thrust obtained is not great but is continuous. This is the only movement in swimming which does not have a recovery phase. Errors that must be corrected include, the hands following a curved track instead of a straight one, the palms out of line with the forearms, and the palms not being held in a flat plane.

When using the breast stroke movement of the legs to keep oneself upright at the surface the thighs should form an angle of 110°–130° with the trunk and the knees should not be too far apart (130). In the recovery stage the feet should remain at an angle to the legs and should be brought slowly as close as possible to the buttocks.

130 *Using the leg stroke to keep afloat.*

The stroke consists of shooting out the legs, during which the soles of the feet provide thrust by pressing down on the water; and at the same time the legs come together which also forces water downwards. This combined effect will not occur if the legs are extended apart and only come together afterwards. To obtain maximum power, the leg extension and their coming together must be one single movement. The recovery movement must be gentle. The start of the stroke comes when the feet are moved downwards and outwards. Make the maximum effort only when about one third of the movements is completed.

When using the breast stroke for normal swimming, if the legs do not produce much effect the arms can make it up because their contribution is always more efficient. In vertical swimming, which is essential for remaining at the surface or for supporting or helping someone else, the thrust comes principally from the legs.

A controlled surface dive

In preparing for a surface dive the body is held at a slight angle to the vertical (131–1). Make a final leg stroke, and at the same time shoot the arms out forward and take a deep breath. This will bring your body horizontal and diving starts at this point. The legs must always be kept together, and now draw them up into the compact position (131–2) while the arms make a powerful thrust which causes the body to revolve into a head down position (131–3). When the trunk reaches the vertical, the legs and body are stretched straight with the feet pointing upwards (131–4). The legs will be partly out of the water and their weight will start the downward movement of the body. The arms shoot out towards the bottom in the first part of a breast stroke to complete the exercise.

The surface dive is correct if the legs come well out of the water, and this indicates that there is no danger of sinking head downwards. There is no need to rush. The movements must be carried out smoothly and gracefully.

If you find difficulty in reaching a vertical position it indicates that, either the leg stroke or the arm stroke was not done efficiently; if you go beyond the vertical it could be because the dive was done in a rush, or else the drawing up and straightening of the legs was started too late; if you tilt to one side it is because the arms were stretched towards the bottom with the hands together or nearly so, whereas they should always be kept apart to ensure stability.

To perfect this vertical position it is a good idea to practice in water just a little shallower than one's own height. Carry out the surface dive and then, with the legs at least half their length out of the water, you can rest your hands on the bottom.

There is no need to be alarmed if you notice water coming from your nose for some time afterwards. It comes from the sinus passages which filled up when you were underwater.

131

Diving in head first

Diving when loaded with equipment poses some fairly serious problems because it tends to add to the instinctive fear of falling. Consequently, simple dives without equipment are a preparation for the more involved ones that will follow.

It is best to start diving by jumping in standing erect as if at attention. The feet should project by about one-third the edge of the take-off point; one must jump forward a little, but not so far that balance is lost, and look straight ahead. Start from a low height and then, when confidence is gained, increase this to about 2 or 3 meters.

Next try a head first dive which is more difficult. The take-off position is the same, but this time let yourself fall forward, bending only at the waist, with the arms stretched above the head (133). To make sure that the arms and head go in first it is essential to aim for a position not more than one meter ahead of the point of take-off and to keep the legs at all times rigidly straight.

When this is mastered try starting the dive with a jump (134); the only difference is that now the legs act like a spring. When you fall the legs swing upwards taking the pelvis upwards with them. A common fault of beginners is to enter the water with the legs bent. Practice holding them stiffly together and tensed and on taking off point the feet and toes (132).

132

133

134

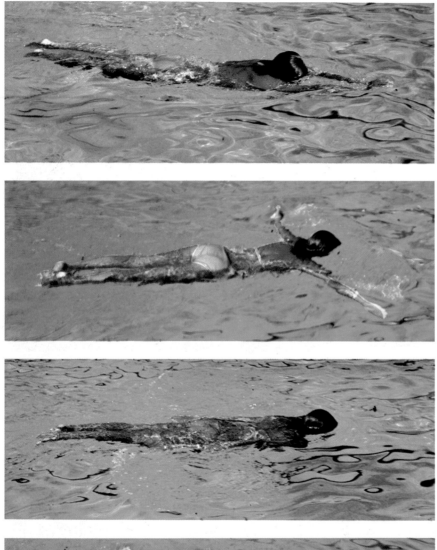

The underwater breast stroke

Contrary to what has been said about the breast stroke on the surface, when swimming underwater the movements of the arms and legs do not have to coincide with breathing, and different techniques can be used. The most common is called the double-strike method and involves two distinct thrusts.

The necessary co-ordination is easy to master and can be tried out initially either on the surface or underwater by carrying out the following movements: Place yourself face downwards with the arms extended in front of you and the legs close together stretched out with the feet pointed (135). Start by sweeping the arms apart and back until they reach your sides thus carrying out a stroke with the arms which is followed by a pause while the forward momentum lasts (136, 137). As soon as the speed drops you must simultaneously bring forward both the legs and the arms (138). When the arms are fully extended start the normal leg stroke. This second phase gives less forward thrust because the recovery phase will have a braking effect, and so there will also be a shorter pause before making the stroke.

Bending at the waist in this horizontal position will cause the thighs to give the main braking effect. In this recovery movement the main bend should therefore be mostly at the knees and as little as possible at the waist.

The breast stroke action can be done in exactly the same way when the swimmer is on her back (139, 140).

135 to 138 *The breast stroke.*

139 140 *The breast stroke done on the back.*

Swimming on the surface

The fastest method of swimming is the crawl which uses a short, rapid and rhythmical beat with the legs stretched and the feet extended (141). The legs make three beats for each time a hand comes out of the water; that is, on each stroke. It is the thigh that produces the stroke, consequently the movement comes from the hip and not the knee. It is a serious fault to bend the knees voluntarily or to allow them to bend too much (145). To avoid this, beginners should hold the legs rigid, since this is better than too much bend.

The good swimmer remains horizontal in the water and never raises his head; it is only turned sideways for breathing. The speed in fact creates a hollow in the wave alongside the head, and so it is possible to breathe from below the water surface level (142).

It is very difficult to correct quickly the other common mistakes unless the position of the body, and the breathing which is connected with it, is got right first.

Beginners are unable to go fast enough, and so must breathe at the surface of the water in such a way as to raise the head as little as possible. Raising the head cause the body to become tensed and the legs will sink (143). It is essential to stay level with the head immersed up to the hair. In order to breathe, the head is turned without raising it, and this will be possible with the ear and the temple still under water.

Turning the head on its own, even when in this correct position, is not enough to bring the mouth to the surface of the water. Advantage must also be taken of the sideways movements of the body caused by the arm which is swinging forward on recovery.

In practicing the crawl slowly and smoothly the correct rhythm is one complete breath for every two arm strokes, so that a breath is always taken on the same side. Start to inhale when the arm begins to come out of the water, because the body has then already begun its sideways displacement (142). The breath must cease when the arm ap-

141 142 *The crawl.*

proaches the vertical in the middle of the recovery, because by then the body will already have started to return to the level position. Start breathing out immediately, because otherwise the lungs cannot be emptied, even though there is more time for breathing out than there is for breathing in.

So blow out at once as soon as the inward breath has ceased and this is done with the mouth wide open, and later on through the mouth and the nose, but never through the nose alone.

The arm recovery is through the air, and is therefore quicker than the stroke which is through water. Consequently the arm which is entering the water cannot start the stroke immediately but must wait until the stroke of the other arm is completed. The hand, therefore, shoots forward and sinks gently into the water for 8 to 12 inches with the fingers pointed ahead and down. The arm enters the water first with the fingers, then the wrist and finally the elbow. It is a mistake to place the hand level since it then strikes the water and is lifted, so resisting its forward movement.

Each hand must enter the water directly in front of its own shoulder (141). If it enters too near the center line of the body an oscillation will be set up due to the sideways movement of the pelvis; on the other hand if it enters too far out or too early (144) the body will oscillate due to the sideways movement of the shoulders. Ragged movements and oscillation will reduce speed. Finally, when making the stroke, the palm of the hand must press against the water for the whole of its arc right back to the thighs.

143   *Raising the head too far.*

144   *Sideways oscillation.*

145   *Too much knee bend.*

Swimming techniques with basic equipment

146 *For snorkeling one only needs basic equipment.*

Basic equipment includes a simple breathing tube which allows one to breathe with the face submerged; fins which will increase swimming speed, even when used incorrectly; a mask which protects the eyes and the nose passages from the water while allowing good visibility (146).

If the water temperature at the surface is less than about 20°C (68°F), the time has come to put on a wet-suit. A wet-suit is not recommended for the first attempts at swimming underwater which have just been discussed because it increases the physical effort required and hinders the uncertain movements of the beginner. It is not usually necessary in a swimming pool but should be considered for all open water situations where a temperature of less than 20°C (68°F) is anticipated.

Everything about diving is very different when using equipment but, on the other hand the range of possibilities is greater and one has control over the conditions, particularly if the recommended

type of suit is used and the diver trained to use it. When putting on a wet-suit it is better to take your watch off. If the suit goes on easily there is no problem, but if not sprinkle the inside with talcum powder. With lined suits there is usually no difficulty.

If the temperature is not too cold the wet-suit can be put on while in the water where the water film will form a lubricant between the skin and the neoprene and thus help with the fitting. If there is an uncomfortable delay between putting the suit on and starting to dive and if it has an integral hood, this can be pulled back without any difficulty.

The amount of weight to carry is first

estimated, and can be adjusted later from the results of the dive. Only add the minimum weights to start with. If using a wet-suit, fins, mask and snorkel, adjust the weights when in the water, after having taken a breath, until a balance is reached which is similar to the same buoyancy that the naked body has on its own. If a deep dive is planned it is advisable to carry a little less weight because at greater depths the overall weight will increase owing to the decrease in the thickness of the wet-suit and the reduced volume of the body under the increased pressure.

When wearing breathing apparatus the same procedure is carried out but in

147   *Clearing the mask.*

148   *Removing a fin.*

addition one has to add as many kilograms (or pounds) as the weight of air which will be used up from the tanks during the course of the dive.

Putting on the mask and snorkel
These items are prepared ashore. Adjust the strap of the mask so that it is not too tight and fasten it. To prevent fogging of the face plate, spit on the inside; spread this evenly over the glass, and then rinse off.

The projecting flanges of the snorkel mouthpiece are placed between the lips and the gums; the two stem pieces are held between the teeth—but take care not to bite into them.

The mask strap goes around the back of the head and the mask is placed just under the nose; smooth out any wrinkles, then check that no hair is caught between the rubber seal and the forehead. In use, the snorkel should normally be upright, except when looking towards the bottom. There will be times when water will get into the mask. Clear it when on the surface in this way: breathe in and then, with one hand pressing the top of the mask firmly onto the forehead, breathe out through the nose (147). The water which is at the bottom will be forced out together with the rush of escaping air. The snorkel tube may also fill with water and can be cleared with a sharp puff of

air. Learn to clear the snorkel by practicing when ashore to blow air sharply, just like firing a pea from a pea-shooter.

Putting on fins
This can be done either in the water or on land, standing or sitting, but the fins should be wet so that the feet slide in easily. Generally one works the feet as far into place as possible and then the heel can be pulled on with the fingers. To take them off while standing on the ground fold back the heel of the fin and then hold it down by standing on the blade. The foot can now be pulled out (148).

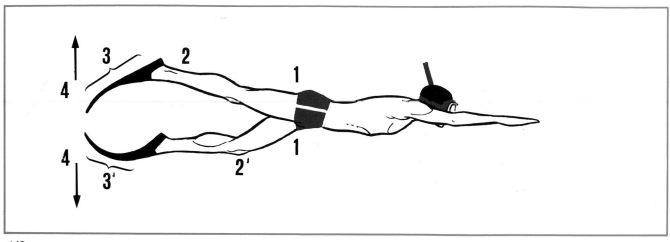

149

Using fins, right and wrong

When using a fin correctly (149) it acts like the tail of a fish. It always gives positive thrust and pushes against the water with its back (–3') and then the sole (–3) alternately. The leg movement is the same as in the crawl; the movement should be a large one and fairly slow and comes from the thigh and not the lower leg. Only slight bending of the knee (–2') should be allowed and then only on account of the resistance the fin meets when thrusting with its back. The feet should always be extended. Correct use of the fin forces the legs to oscillate like pendulums (–4) and at the extremes of their swings they should be at least three feet apart. This large oscillation is important as fins of the current type only give full thrust when the blade is curved correctly at the limit of each swing. At each changeover between swings there is a dead point where there is no thrust and as a result the shorter the swing of the leg the greater is the proportion of time with no power output.

The fins will not work properly if the bend at the knee is too great (150–2'). In such cases the angle of the upper part, or back, of the fin will not be correct and it will simply slide through the water and give no forward thrust. This is also likely to be the case when it is pushed with the sole and the foot is not stretched out straight (151–3).

Mistakes in using fins

If fins are badly used both the recovery and the stroke will be affected and consequently the thrust will not be constant. There are two types of common mistakes made by swimmers when using fins: these

150

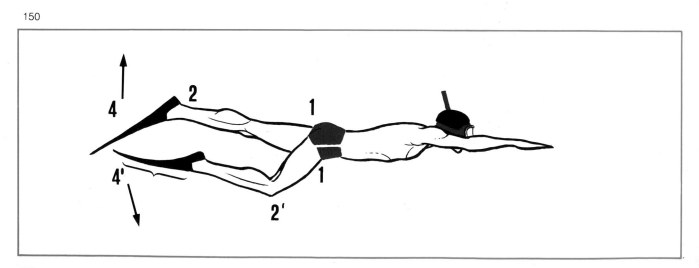

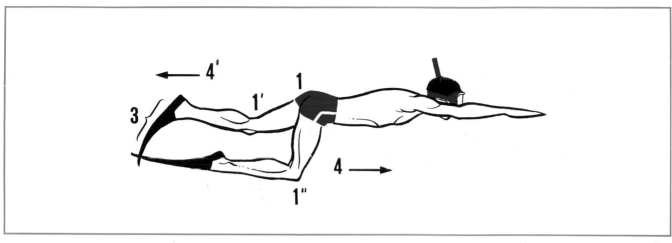

151

are known as the *bicycle* and the *water kick*. In the bicycle (151) the legs are bent both at the hip (–1) and at the knee (–1' and –1''). Thus the fin instead of producing a powerful thrust from its return stroke, simply makes what is in effect a recovery stroke which is neutral. Moreover the other part of the stroke is wrong since the resistance of the water turns the foot so that the fin only presses with the sole flat (–3) instead of flicking like a fish-tail.

In the *water kick* the reverse happens (152). The legs bend only at the knee (–1

and 1'), so that, at the moment when the sole of the fin ought to be delivering thrust (–4), it is in fact completely passive, making, in effect, a recovery. To make the stroke, the leg has to straighten and the water resistance bends back the foot which gives a certain amount of thrust (–4').

Learn the right way
It is no good trying to learn simply by enjoying the extra speed that even a bad technique can give. The best learning method is to weigh oneself with 3 to 4

kilograms and then to set oneself vertically in the water without a mask (153). Hold the legs stiff and practice a slow, steady rhythm just sufficient to keep the mouth clear of the water. The stroke and return should take the feet as wide apart as possible.

You will almost certainly find that there is some unevenness in your strokes, caused possibly by one leg being stronger than the other and in consequence there will be a tendency to turn. Practice controlling this tendency and then try to turn on purpose by using the hands. You will

152

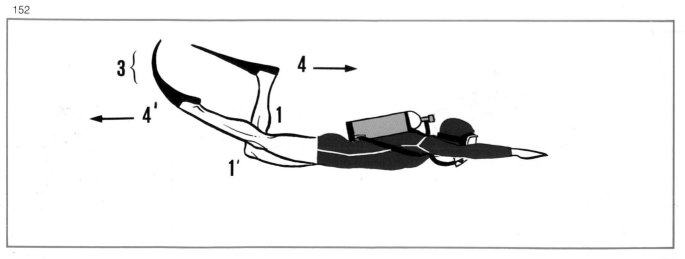

need to be able to do this when re-surfacing at a later stage.

When you are confident that your stroke and control are good you can try the side-stroke in which the lower arm is stretched out ahead and the other lies along the side of the body (154). Only raise your head the minimum necessary to breathe. This style permits the fins to be separated the widest possible amount without causing splashing or noise. Concentrate now on perfecting the fin strokes particularly as to their accuracy, rhythm, balance and the greatest leg separation before moving on to the commonly used styles.

The back stroke is the best for long distances (155). The amplitude of the leg swing will have to be slightly reduced but the rate can be increased to keep up the speed. The classic position for the body is as if one was almost impercepti-bly seated. You can regulate this with your head. With the chin held down on the chest the body will tilt diagonally towards the bottom; raising the chin and bending the head backwards will cause the body to come to the surface. The position is correct when the fins form whirlpools but do not quite break surface.

When swimming in a head up position on the surface (156), in order to breathe you must hold the legs well stretched. The extent of the leg movements will have to be reduced in order to keep the fins submerged and it will also be neces-sary to tilt the body slightly. When swim-ming under water this problem does not arise.

153   *Practicing the fin stroke.*

154   *The side stroke with fins.*

155 *The back stroke with fins.*

156 *The fin stroke with head up.*

157

A surface dive with fins

When wearing equipment, including a snorkel, the starting position is horizontal (157), the same as for the controlled surface dive without fins. A rolling dive should begin with a well-timed thrust (Position 1) and while the body is turning towards the vertical position bring the legs together and close to the body (Positions 2 and 3) then bend at the waist and stretch the legs upwards (159, Position 1). If the legs go beyond the vertical the cause is either that the starting impulse was too violent or that the legs were raised too late or both faults together. If, on the other hand, they do not reach the vertical, either the initial thrust or the downward bend or both were insufficient.

A right-angle dive from the surface is done with the legs stretched out (158, Position 1). It is much the same as the rolling dive with a few additions. In this method the legs are raised up while stretched out straight by a decisive effort of the back and stomach muscles and thus their weight tends to pull the trunk back from its vertical position. Therefore either the arms must counter this by thrusting in an opposite direction or else it must be balanced by a certain amount of initial impetus.

The important things to note are that in turning the body to make a head-down dive, the critical position for the body to reach is with the legs vertical, held together, stretched out and with the feet (or fins) extended, and secondly that one should not start to use the fins until they are well below the surface (160).

Beginners, when using weights, should not attempt to turn head down on the surface but dive by sinking naturally. The first two methods are only useful when one wants to travel forward at the same time.

158

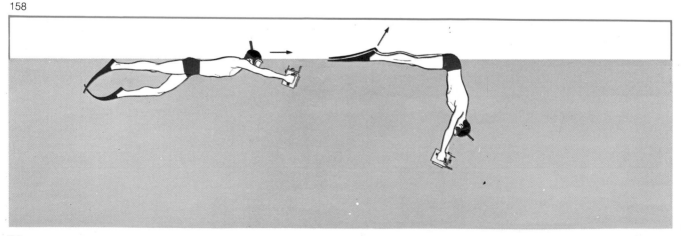

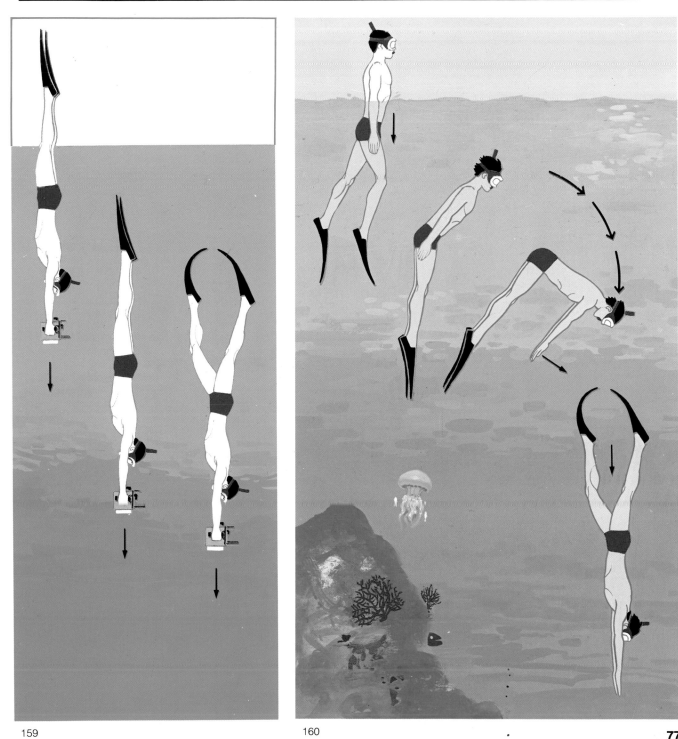

159

160

SWIMMING TECHNIQUES WITH BASIC EQUIPMENT

Entering the water

Never jump in from too great a height when wearing any equipment. Start first from a low staging using the methods already described. From low levels (and also from heights) one usually jumps while holding oneself perfectly erect (161). Always have one hand on the mask, with the palm covering the front of the eyepiece and the fingers firmly grasping the rim. If you want to limit the depth reached you jump in the scissors position (162), with the legs held straight but as far apart as possible and they are brought forcibly together on entering the water.

From a boat, however, if the sides are not too high, one can enter the water by means of the backward roll. Sit on the edge with the buttocks projecting outboard and roll over into the water backwards (163). The body must be bent at an angle of less than 90° and the legs must be fully stretched out; otherwise the legs or the heels may strike the edge of the boat and be injured.

161 162

163

First lessons in diving

To stay on the bottom a diver must be ballasted. A guide to the weight of ballast needed is just enough to allow him to sink after having taken a breath. When on the bottom there are two standard positions. Either:

- facing the bottom with legs stretched apart, feet extended and forearms resting on the bottom;
- kneeling with the legs placed to form an equilateral triangle and with the flippers resting lightly on the bottom and the body leaning slightly backwards (164).

Practice clearing the mask. It will have to be done later on during diving and so now is the time to become accustomed to the strong inrush of water into the eyes and nose passages (164). Start by kneeling and looking downward, first ease the mask away from the face so that it fills with water. The mask is then replaced and, looking slightly upwards, hold the sides with both hands and press firmly on the part which seals against the forehead. At the same time ease the pressure on the bottom edge along the upper lip. Blowing out through the nose will now empty the mask.

Many of the preceding exercises concern things which are not normally needed for ordinary snorkeling, but to face having to do them later by chance without previous practice is another matter. However, there are many people who find that if they have to undertake an unaccustomed and difficult job, they possess a great deal more stamina than they normally have when doing something less active. Without the stimulus of mental effort there is time for fear or apprehension.

A beginner should not make snorkel dives that are too long or he may find himself becoming hyperventilated; he must always be on the lookout for this. It is not wise to start by taking the deepest possible breath because this puts all the muscles associated with breathing under stress (166). However, filling the lungs to the maximum can be used for deep dives since the hydrostatic pressure reduces the volume of gas in the lungs and thus eases the tension of the muscles in the chest and diaphragm.

At the first sign of spasms of the diaphragm a diver should come to the surface calmly and resume breathing normally. This is a test which inexperienced divers should not take too far.

A good exercise in self-control is to weight oneself and then put on some other equipment which has previously been placed on the bottom. Try this first at a depth of about 6 feet (2 meters)

164   *Clearing the mask.*

166   *Practicing self-control.*

165

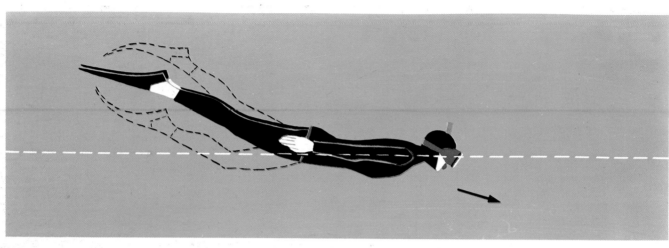

167

(165). Put on the fins and the face mask. Then empty the mask and return to the surface.

Some exercises should be performed without weights; in these one cannot merely sink but must use the head-down surface dive. When doing this use both the rolling method and the right-angle dive to keep in practice. To perfect and maintain the correct techniques they must become instinctive so that no energy or time is wasted when there are more important things to concentrate on.

An exercise for perfecting underwater swimming is to go for considerable distances horizontally at a constant depth of not more than 10 feet (3 meters). Then do the same with the weight adjusted first to give you positive buoyancy and then negative.

To overcome positive buoyancy when horizontal (167) the body should be bent slightly at the waist, which has the effect of making the fins operate a little higher than the head and thus give a forward and downward thrust. On the other hand to counter negative buoyancy the legs must operate below the horizontal plane (168). Arch the back to force the fins down and you will find yourself moving gently diagonally towards the surface.

168

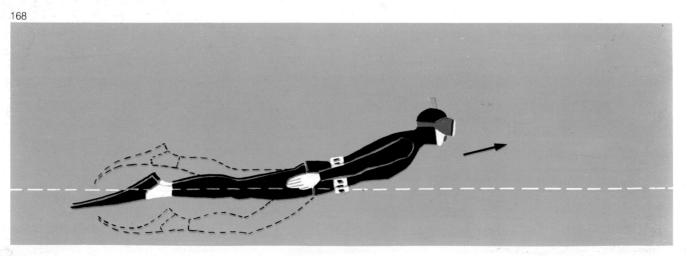

169 *During a deep snorkel attempt.*

Techniques for snorkel divers

Snorkelers comprise a large proportion of divers, and it is here that one finds the greatest number of young people. This branch of diving is as far as most people care to go and one only needs to be an ordinary swimmer and to carry the barest essentials of equipment. However, even though the dangers for a snorkel-diver are less in number than those for a diver with breathing equipment, the risk is not in fact less. A snorkel-diver sometimes has only a very brief period available to him for reacting to an emergency situation. For this reason even a simple error or a moment's inattention can be serious.

On the surface
When swimming on the surface and watching the sea floor, a diver is face down and in this position it is not easy to keep his fins underwater. The stroke, therefore, cannot be very powerful and it is difficult to avoid splashing. A possible solution is to swim partially on one's side, though this reduces the field of view somewhat. If it is not necessary to look at the bottom, especially if long distances have to be covered, the best way to swim is on the back. As usual the body should be relaxed and the breathing deep and calm.

170 *Practicing clearing the ears.*

The descent

Before going down, the diver should make a brief hyperventilation of the lungs and take a maximum breath, followed immediately by a surface dive. Perfect technique here should be the aim and this is not only a matter of style—it is by far the most effective. For a fast descent the arms should do nothing. To try to use them would only cause resistance and spoil the streamlining, and so they must be held close along the body or stretched out ahead. The fin movement must be as wide as possible, the speed of the beat being varied according to the power required.

During the first part of the descent a free diver is more or less buoyant, which produces an upward thrust; this has to be opposed by propelling oneself down with the flippers. In the later stages of the descent he is in a state of more and more negative buoyancy, which aids his progress. This is important because during the course of a dive, whether free-diving or with breathing equipment, a diver must constantly aim to conserve his energy.

It is essential to clear the ears frequently (170) in order to avoid a buildup of pressure which would result in bursting the eardrum. Each time this is done the balance must be restored completely. Partial clearing is not enough. Perfect balance is reached when both eardrums feel as though they are being pulled slightly outwards. They may not in fact come into balance at the same moment because the two tubes will react differently. On reaching the bottom the diver should always clear his ears again to make certain of equal pressures outside and in.

After making the surface dive the snorkel is of no further use and so the mouthpiece may be spat out. If returning to the surface it is necessary to keep watch below it can be brought back into action very easily. In case of trouble, however, one can always break surface and breathe air normally and thus avoid having to blow to clear the tube. If surface conditions are rough it is advisable to retain the snorkel in the mouth throughout the dive.

171 *Moving among eel-grass with weights and a safety line.*

Behavior on the bottom

Snorkel-diving must always be supervised by someone on the surface and the return to the surface must always start when there is still plenty of safety margin, which depends on the distance to be covered. During these short dives a snorkel-diver has to adjust his activities, whether it is swimming, exploring, collecting, or hunting, according to the visibility and the characteristics of the sea bed; this should always be with the greatest caution. If the bottom is sandy it may seem to be free of any hidden danger, but a snorkel-diver can easily become tangled, say, in a nylon net which may be practically invisible (173). On a seabed with many obstructions, nets and long thin fishing lines (174), which are tough and elastic, are frequently met and difficult to see. To be caught when one's margin of time is almost ended can be serious.

On rocky bottoms one often comes across gullies with narrow clefts or overhanging projections (172) and in the neighborhood of breakwaters natural and artificial rocks may be stacked at random. These are obvious hazards where the greatest care is necessary. When penetrating gaps under rocks, if one has positive buoyancy go in face upwards so that one can pull oneself ahead by clinging to the roof. If buoyancy is negative, do the opposite.

Resurfacing

There are two particular points to be considered: the first is the departure from the seabed, which must begin with plenty of time left; the second is the ascent itself which may be normal or emergency.

84

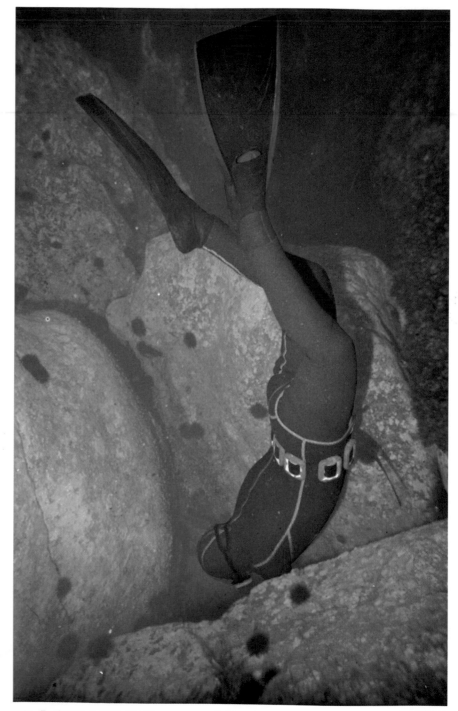

172 *Exploring a cave mouth.*

173   *Beware of nets which are almost invisible.*

174   *A snorkeler can be caught by a fishing line.*

85

TECHNIQUES FOR SNORKEL DIVERS

A normal ascent can be done either slowly or fast. It is usually advisable to slow down for the final approach to the surface when the diver is only carried up by his normal buoyancy. One must not forget that there is always a risk of colliding with a propeller (noisy) or else against a sailing or a rowboat (silent) and remember that apart from injuries themselves, even a simple mishap underwater, can sometimes be enough to cause drowning.

If you are in any doubt pull yourself up along the mooring rope of the diver's marker buoy (175) or come up with one arm stretched out ahead to explore the surface (176), and turn in a spiral fashion at the same time.

175

Problems

When surfacing in emergencies there are various possibilities. In the rare case of a minor accident or illness one must use the fins normally, remaining relaxed but increasing the speed as far as possible without losing control. Keep the arms and the hands against the thighs.

If there is a fear of a blackout caused by holding the breath too long, go for the surface fast. It is essential, however, not to lose control since panic can cause muscle spasms or induce the diver to use his arms, increasing the oxygen consumption without any real advantage.

Loss of consciousness associated with an over long snorkel-dive can be classified as controlled or emergency, simple or complicated. The condition is controlled when the diver is at a shallow depth and can interrupt the dive by returning to the surface when he wishes. It is an emergency, on the other hand, when the diver wants to cut short the dive but the distance or some obstacle prevents him from reaching the surface in time.

In the first case the diver is calm and the eventual loss of consciousness is simple since he will have kept his mouth closed when completing the dive. In the second case he can panic and open his mouth in a desperate attempt to breathe. Consequently he will inhale water and the blackout will be complicated by the start of true drowning. Worse than that, he may find himself in a state of negative buoyancy because he will have exhaled all his air and there will be less chance of recovering him and reviving him.

Self-control is vital for a diver. It is acquired by practice. A good guide to success is in being able to think as calmly at the end of a dive as at the beginning.

Having surfaced, it is best to hyperventilate the lungs as soon as possible in order to restore the body condition to normal. In any case, leave plenty of time for recuperation before attempting to go down again.

176

177 *A snorkeler's catch.*

3 Diving with Breathing Equipment

Special problems for SCUBA divers

Range of operation

Self-contained underwater breathing apparatus (SCUBA) has a limited range, unlike the diving bell or the 'standard dress' supplied by an air hose from an almost inexhaustible source. This range depends on a variety of factors, none of which is fixed. For example; the amount of air carried in the tanks; the temperature of the water; and the physical effort which a man must expend during the dive.

In fact the internal pressure in the cylinder measured at the temperature of the outside air can be quite different when submerged in water. Heat loss, as well as the even more significant differences in physical effort, mean that a diver's consumption of air can be higher than expected and hard to predict accurately. Moreover a diver is rarely able to comply with an exact schedule especially when it is remembered that his air endurance at the surface is reduced to a half at 10 meters, to a third at 20 meters and to a quarter at 30 meters. In practice, therefore, any calculation which is made has to have a large margin built in for safety.

When swimming on the surface without any particular objective a man will use about 25 liters of air per minute; at 10 meters, 50 liters; at 20 meters, 75 liters, and at 30 meters, 100 liters. Added to this it must be remembered that beginners will use more because their relative lack of expertise and poor technique mean that they will make unnecessary and clumsy movements which will increase the need for air.

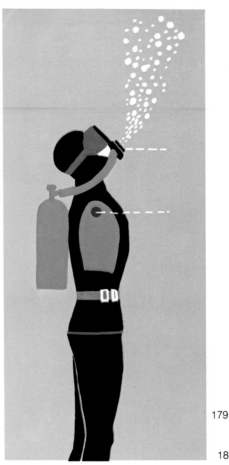

179

180

Breathing effort

When breathed underwater, air is compressed and hence denser and heavier, since it contains more molecules per unit volume. At 10 meters for example, the pressure has doubled, and so air of the same volume contains twice as many molecules as it would on the surface.

At the surface 1 liter of air weighs 1.25 grams; at 10 meters, 2.50 grams; at 30 meters, 5 grams. To pass this denser air through the bronchial passages needs a greater effort from the breathing muscles. At 30 meters the maximum volume per minute by which a diver can expand his lungs is only half that at the surface. This reduction in efficiency means in effect that, for example, at 30 meters the maximum volume per minute a diver can breathe is half of that which is possible on the surface.

It is not only the density of the gas which causes extra effort in breathing. To draw air from the regulator the diver has to make a positive effort to suck the valve open. Another point is the position of the regulator in relation to the body's breathing system. They rarely coincide, so that if the regulator is higher (179) the effort needed to expand the chest and draw in air is greater, whereas if it is lower (180) extra force is needed to breathe out.

If one adds up all these small items and also takes into account the higher density of the gas mixture, it can be understood how even a small physical effort can become a serious undertaking. Lack of skill can lead to shortage of breath and thus to the urgent need to breathe deeply and frequently, which increases consumption. Taken on its own the rate of consumption of air is only something to be watched and allowed for. Breathing difficulty, however, is the result of the sum of many small things and, in turn, it becomes the cause of others.

A summary of the factors contributing to this difficulty includes the following:

- increase in the density of the gas mixture relative to the depth;
- the vertical distance between the center of the lungs and the regulator;
- an increase in the output of the body's temperature regulation system due to lower temperatures;
- resistance to movement caused by the increased density of the surrounding water or to stiffness in the texture of the wet-suit;
- fatigue of the muscles used in swimming or in working;
- emotion, anxiety, panic;
- excessive difficulty in managing the equipment;
- conditions of positive or negative buoyancy which require additional effort and movement to remain in the required position (181).

Breathlessness must be absolutely avoided and, particularly in deep water, the diver must constantly be in total control of his breathing. If control starts to be lost it must be regained at once. If it is impossible to do so, return to the surface should be immediate.

A rare danger in diving with breathing equipment is a blocking of the valve in the regulator. This can be serious since it may cut off the air supply if it occurs just after the diver has exhaled. The depth at which one finds oneself and the extent of the eventual air shortage governs the chance of surfacing before blacking out. Furthermore, especially in a case of panic, resurfacing at high speed in such a condition brings a danger of over-expansion of the lungs, which can lead to air embolism. Further complications are an uncontrolled ascent which does

181 *With positive buoyancy it is an effort to keep on the bottom.*

not lie within the limits of the safety curve (*see this page*) and also the possibility of obstacles or dangers on the surface.

The safety curve

We have limited ourselves so far to dives which permit a direct ascent without a pause—that is to say, within the safety curve (182-185). The graphs show how much time a diver can spend at various depths without being obliged to wait before surfacing. The time is calculated from the moment at which the diver leaves the surface (the start of the increase in pressure) until the moment at which he starts his ascent (the start of the decrease in pressure). This figure is not easy to work out since it can vary frequently, especially with sport diving. The only way for a beginner to avoid making a mistake is to treat the whole of the dive as though it had taken place at the maximum depth reached.

Decompression tables

Anyone who goes beyond the limits of the safety curve has to follow the decompression tables and must make a stop before surfacing (187) or risk an embolism. If the extent of the dive requires stops to be made, then any incident which would require rapid resurfacing

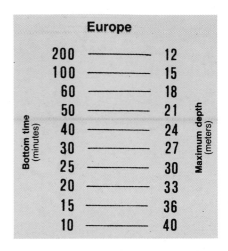

Europe	
Bottom time (minutes)	Maximum depth (meters)
200	12
100	15
60	18
50	21
40	24
30	27
25	30
20	33
15	36
10	40

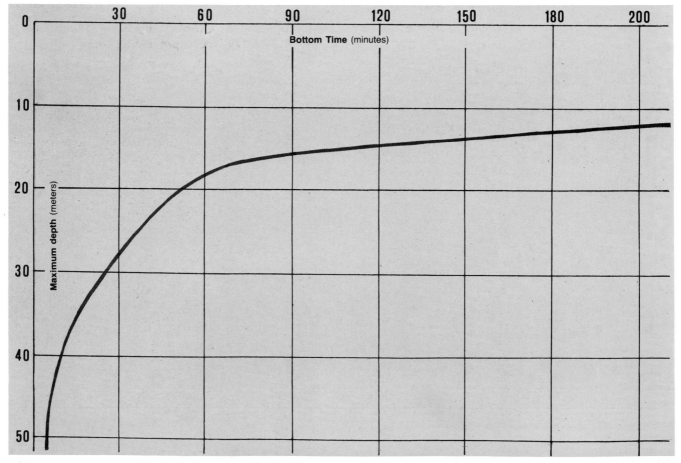

Great Britain
RNPL/BSAC

Maximum Depth (metres)	Bottom Time (Minutes)
9	No limit
10	232
12	137
14	96
16	72
18	57
20	46
22	38
24	32
26	27
28	23
30	20

183

United States
U.S. Navy

Maximum Depth (feet)	Bottom Time (minutes)
30	No limit
40	200
50	100
60	60
70	50
80	40
90	30
100	25

184

will cause serious complications. Therefore a novice diver must never go beyond the curve while he is inexperienced. However, it is quite easy accidentally to pass beyond the curve by a small amount either from not taking enough care or from too much or too prolonged physical effort. When there is any doubt of having made a mistake, a stop of a least 5 minutes at a depth of 5 meters should be made before resurfacing.

In general one can say that the stages of decompression are stops of suitable duration which become more prolonged as the diver nears the surface and are made every 5 meters (every 10 feet in U.S. Navy tables) for ease of calculation.

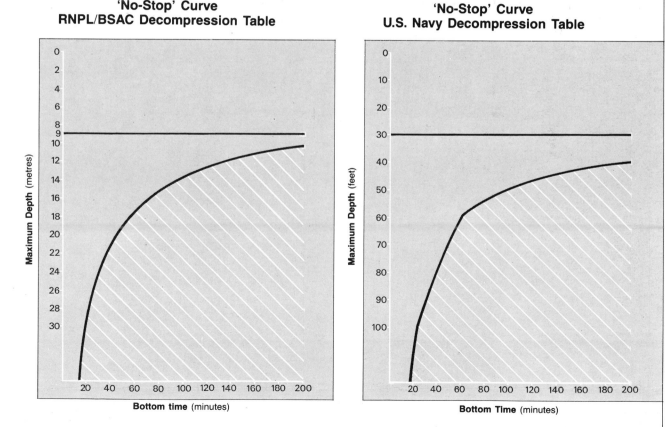

185

SPECIAL PROBLEMS FOR SCUBA DIVERS

The deeper and longer the dive the more frequent and lengthy are the decompression stops. For example, after spending 30 minutes at 30 meters a diver might stop for 5 minutes at 10 meters and 10 minutes at 5 meters. Note that the stops are longer at the shallower end which is where the changes in volume of the gas are greatest compared with change in depth. In the U.K. it is customary to use the tables of the Royal Navy, while divers in the U.S. use those of the U.S. Navy.

Compact new dive planners have been developed for recreational diving: some are in table form; there is also a wheel which is easier to use and allows for multilevel dives.

186 187 *Divers at a decompression stage.*

SPECIAL PROBLEMS FOR SCUBA DIVERS

Decompression problems

An embolism is an example of the application of Henry's Law, which states that the amount of gas (that is, its weight) that will dissolve in a liquid at a given temperature is almost directly proportional to its partial pressure. Oxygen and carbon dioxide are involved in the exchange of gases within the cells and so, since they do not accumulate, they are not a problem as regards embolism. Nitrogen, however, which is an inert gas, is transferred to the blood via the lung membranes (alveoli) and then accumulates in the system. At sea level the human body contains about 1 liter of nitrogen in solution.

As has been previously explained, descent below the surface causes the hydrostatic pressure to be added to the atmospheric pressure by one atmosphere for every 10 meters of depth. So at 10 meters the total absolute pressure is 2 ATA and if the diver remains for 12 hours at this depth an additional liter of nitrogen will pass into solution in his body. If he then descends from 10 meters to 20 and stays for a further 12 hours another liter will be dissolved, and yet another if he descends to 30 meters staying there a further 12 hours. Therefore at 30 meters his body will contain in solution, in addition to the 1 liter normally found at sea level, 3 liters of nitrogen which have been dissolved during the three periods

of 12 hours at each stage.

If, however, the diver was to go from the surface directly to 30 meters his body would absorb the same three liters of nitrogen all in the space of 12 hours. This is because the speed at which gas is dissolved is proportional to the difference in pressure between the gas under pressure and the gas in solution.

The normal length of the type of dive we are concerned with is short so that a state of total saturation will never be reached. Certain parts of the body may become totally saturated with nitrogen, blood for example, whereas others will only have dissolved a negligible amount, such as bone. In any case, all ascents from deep water to atmospheric pressure must be controlled and never be allowed to go too fast, since this could easily cause the formation of emboli consisting of bubbles of free nitrogen which form in the tissues.

One can easily imagine what happens by thinking of a bottle of champagne. This contains a gas dissolved in the liquid but no bubbles can be seen (189). If, however, we take out the cork, the pressure which was present in the neck of the bottle is replaced by the much lower atmospheric pressure and the gas is liberated from the wine in the form of a mass of foaming bubbles (190). Something of the kind happens to our bodies

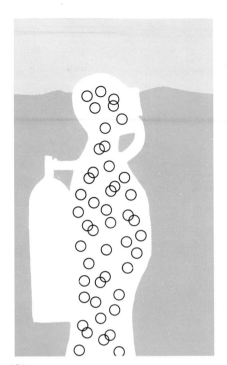

191

192

189

190

when rising from deep water to the surface which is at atmospheric pressure (191, 192).

Some tissues release gas at a greater rate than others and this depends on the pressure which the nitrogen has been able to reach by that time in each of them. For example, in the slow absorbing tissues, the pressure rise may be negligible. Blood, however, can easily become saturated and also can release the nitrogen rapidly, and we find the same type of bubble formation as in the bottle of champagne.

To summarize, therefore, we should note that the human body can withstand an increase in the external pressure (that is why no special care need be taken on the descent), but it cannot freely withstand a reduction in the outside pressure, such as occurs in an uncontrolled ascent.

If the limits of the safety curve are crossed it is essential to avoid the formation of nitrogen bubbles and so the ascent must be slow or else stopped near the surface (187-196) to allow the tissues to transfer the nitrogen to the blood. The blood passes continuously through the network of capillaries in the surface of the lungs which will then carry the excess nitrogen away outside the body via the mouth and nose.

Unless the correct routine is carried out the bubbles of nitrogen that form in the tissues will become too large and then the body is unable either to tolerate them or eliminate them.

The condition resulting from a pressure-induced irregularity is known as a barotrauma.

Barotraumas can be roughly separated into two groups which relate to the mistakes in procedure of two types of diver: those that arise from a too rapid ascent or a serious error in decompression stops even after a fairly short and shallow dive; and those that affect people working in pressure chambers or professional divers who stay for long periods at high pressures but return to atmospheric pressure very slowly when the decompression is carried out in a diving bell or in a decompression chamber.

193 *Diver about to break surface.*

SPECIAL PROBLEMS FOR SCUBA DIVERS

The symptoms of the first group, depending on where the bubbles are found, are as follows:
- bubbles in the chest: pain in the chest, breathlessness, pain in the heart;
- bubbles in the brain: loss of consciousness, general weakness, disturbances of vision, or sudden blindness, disturbances of speech, giddiness, paralysis of one or more limbs;
- bubbles in the spinal cord: pain in the back, tingling, lack of feeling, weakness, loss of control or paralysis of the lower limbs, blocking of the intestines or the bladder.

The symptoms of the second group, again according to the location of the bubbles, are as follows:
- bubbles in the inner ear: dizziness nausea, vomiting, loss of balance;
- bubbles in the joints, bones and ligaments: pain in the bones and in the joints, particularly at the knees, elbows and shoulders;
- bubbles in the subcutaneous tissues: itching, alteration in the color of the skin with white, scarlet and livid stains.

The type of embolism in the first group, which is the more serious, will show its symptoms within the space of a few minutes, usually within a quarter of an hour. A typical habit of old divers was for them to remain at the ladder, after removing their helmets, long enough to smoke a cigarette, before climbing back into the boat (194). If any symptoms arose they put their helmets on again and descended rapidly to recompress and so dissipate the embolism.

Pains in the limbs and joints resulting from bubble formation are given the name 'bends'.

In the case of an embolism there is only one truly effective cure, which is to recompress and then to dissipate it by slow decompression, not usually by diving again as was done at one time, but in a modern decompression chamber (195).

A type of embolism which is quite common is due to over-expansion of the lungs;

this has already been described in the chapter concerning the human body in diving. If when ascending the diver does not maintain a balance between the water pressure and the pressure in the lungs, the gas will expand and over-inflate the lung alveoli. If this difference in pressure reaches about two-tenths of an atmosphere the lung tissue will be at bursting point. If it does so the diver suffers what is called an air embolism. This is a serious condition.

The air can thus pass directly into the blood, and from thence to the heart and so into the main arteries. Usually this air, which is in the form of large bubbles, ends up blocking a blood vessel in the brains or in the spinal cord. In one or two minutes at most it will produce disturbances in the nervous system such as those already described and the only effective treatment is to recompress immediately in a pressure chamber.

Nitrogen narcosis
Over the years this condition has been given many names: 'intoxication of the depths,' and 'rapture of the deep' being common.

Opinion is still divided as to the exact cause. However, it has been discovered that nitrogen breathed at high pressure becomes poisonous and upsets the working of the central nervous system. Nowadays, very deep dives carried out by professionals are made using a special mixture where the nitrogen has been replaced by a lighter gas. The partial pressure of the oxygen at these depths has also been reduced quite considerably. Studies recently carried out in the course of dives in which normal air is breathed have suggested that oxygen and carbon dioxide also have an influence on this condition.

Everyone has his own degree of resistance to the effects of the nitrogen intoxication which can be improved by becoming accustomed to it. Divers who are

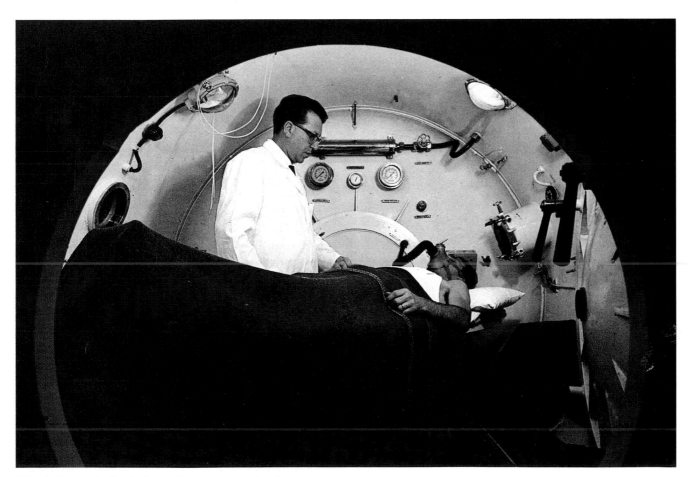

195 *A diver and attendant in a decompression chamber.*

SPECIAL PROBLEMS FOR SCUBA DIVERS

completely inexperienced have felt the effects at about 40 meters after being only 5–10 minutes at that pressure. On the other hand coral divers work as deep as 100 meters breathing air, with dives lasting 10–15 minutes. This is about the limit of their amazing endurance times, which have been built up very gradually during their continuously demanding work.

They also seem to avoid the symptoms of nitrogen narcosis because resistance to it is not constant and varies according to physical condition, which in their case is excellent, and the work which has to be done, which is exacting. Their great experience enables them to maintain perfect self-control and to ascend to a shallower depth the moment they feel the onset of the first symptoms. On reaching a lower pressure the effects of nitrogen narcosis do in fact disappear.

The symptoms of nitrogen narcosis range from an exaggerated sense of well-being, enthusiasm or power, a loss of control, unusual or foolish gestures or behavior, and eventually progress to loss of judgment, slowed reactions, and drunken behavior. There are well-recorded cases of divers who abandoned their group and disappeared towards the bottom without returning and of others who have taken off items of equipment, who have reacted irrationally to recalls and signals, who have knifed their companions or who have gone to sleep on the bottom.

For the most part all this will interest the reader only as information. If he has prepared himself well and makes a slow gradual acclimatization to diving and if he does not go beyond a limit of 15 meters, all will be well. This is in any case a reasonable depth for gaining the basic experience without running undue risks. Of course he should also keep within the limits of the safety curve.

196 *A diver and equipment at a decompression stage.*

197 *Examining plant life when wearing a breathing set.*

SCUBA diving techniques

198

Preparing and putting on the equipment

If the breathing equipment has been exposed to a very high temperature, the pressure in the cylinders must be checked after immersion in water and not in the air. Having connected up the regulator, open the tap to make sure the cylinder is not empty and take one or two breaths through the mouthpiece. This is not so much to check the ease of breathing in but of breathing out. The exhaust valve may be stuck due to age and may have to be cleared. It will avoid trouble later if it is kept lightly lubricated and replaced in time.

If using single-stage apparatus the straps must be accurately adjusted as it is important that the vertical position of the regulator and the center of the lungs should be on the same level when the wearer is standing. If using the two-stage type ensure that the first stage, which often projects considerably, is not pressing on the spine. In both cases the shoulder straps must leave the arms free but

the belt and lower straps must be reasonably tight so that the equipment will stay on the diver's back without slipping.

The wet-suit should be put on even if it is not intended to use it immediately so that an estimate can be made of the weight which will be needed when starting on deeper exercises.

Now start equipping yourself; prepare the mask, fix the knife to the lower leg, stow the snorkel in a safe place, put on the fins, the weight belt and the breathing set (198). The mask is put on just before entering the water.

The breathing set can be put on in various ways depending on the circumstances. The simplest way is to sit down

with it set up behind and then pass the arms through the shoulder straps. However, in order to fasten some types of lower strap one needs to stand up. The set is then put on like a rucksack and if there are several cylinders it will take some doing. One can usually get help but it is better for the diver to learn to be self-sufficient. Another way is to equip oneself in the water standing up on a shallow bottom. In extremely calm sea conditions it is possible to hang the set over the side of the boat and put it on in the water, but this should be left to more experienced divers.

To take the equipment off follow the same procedure in the opposite direction.

Entering the water

Enter the water according to the circumstances and depth by walking or jumping.

It walking one can go in facing the water if it is shallow (199–left). If it is deeper it is better to go in backwards so as to avoid unnecessary hindrance from the fins. If jumping in use one of the methods already described remembering to hold the mask with one hand, to put the thumb of the other hand in the straps pressing them downwards and to look slightly downwards (200).

199

200   *Hold on to the mask and belt when jumping in.*

Basic exercises

The first exercises which the beginner will be taught are those which will allow him to overcome easily the incidents which may occur during his early dives. Armed with these skills he can progress toward complete familiarity with his equipment and its safe use.

In your first lessons try above all else to relax, to breathe slowly and deeply until this becomes automatic. Remember never to hold your breath unnecessarily and particularly when ascending, even in only 2 meters of water, since this can cause an over-expansion of the lungs. This problem is most acute near the surface since the difference in pressure is greatest here.

The first skill to be mastered is that of clearing water from the mouthpiece of the breathing set. Water can enter the mouthpiece in several ways.

- at the beginning of a dive, if you have not entered the water with the mouthpiece already in place;
- during the dive, if for any reason you have had to take the mouthpiece out or had it accidentally knocked out;
- by leakage, if some fault in the regulator is allowing water to enter.

It is inadvisable to attempt to breathe through a mouthpiece which is even partially flooded as the mixture of air and water will irritate the throat and may bring about uncontrollable coughing or choking.

The procedure for clearing the mouthpiece of water is dependent on the type of regulator being used—single hose or twin hose—and whether the diver has just inhaled or exhaled.

A twin-hose (single-stage) regulator has valves set at each side of the mouthpiece along the hose. In most models the air is fed from the regulator along the right-hand hose and is exhausted along the left-hand hose. Any water in the hoses therefore has to follow the same path. To clear the water out simply roll on to your left side, hold the left hose down and the right hose up and blow hard. This should force the water into the left-hand hose and out through the exhaust valve (201). If the diver is swimming horizontally he may find it easier to do a continuous roll

201   *Clearing the hoses by tilting to the left side.*

to the left, breathing out when he turns on his back, which will have the same effect.

If the diver finds that the mouthpiece is flooded when he has already exhaled then he follows a different course. He stands upright, looks up, and removes the mouthpiece. The regulator interprets this action in the same way as an inhalation. The mouthpiece is then turned downward to prevent water flowing back in and the diver lowers it in this position into his mouth, gushing air all the time. This allows the diver to take a deep breath and to follow this with an exhalation which will complete the clearing of water from the hose (202).

With the single-hose (two-stage) type the exhaust valve is situated just below the mouthpiece in the bottom of the regulator casing. Small amounts of water will be expelled automatically if the diver is in any position other than on his back or on his head. If the diver is holding a lungful of air then he has only to place the mouthpiece in his mouth, blow hard, and it will be clear. If, however, he has already exhaled then he must press the button in the center of the front of the regulator casing. This works directly on the diaphragm and will cause a strong blast of air which will clear the water away and allow the diver to breathe.

If a serious defect in the equipment has caused it to malfunction then he will be in one of two situations a free and continuous flow of air from the regulator, or a total lack of air from the regulator. In the first case he must remember that he still has air and can therefore continue to breathe, albeit in a less-controlled way. In the second case he must recognize his condition instantly, check whether he still has his reserve supply and if not, prepare for emergency action. In both cases he must signal to his companion and call for assistance, which will usually take the form of sharing his air supply, or using his spare mouthpiece if he has one.

It is important not to abandon one's

202 *Clearing the mouthpiece of a single-stage breathing set.*

mouthpiece too readily since it may still offer the best alternative (203). A small amount of water may find its way into the mouthpiece if you have been in a head-down position for a long time or if the low temperature has made your lips numb. This can be cleared easily and is not a problem. If the regulator gets 'tight' and gives air grudgingly then this is a sign that the air is almost exhausted; in this case, if you start your return to the surface immediately you will find the lessening pressure releases sufficient air for a safe ascent.

It is important to practice clearing water from the mask while wearing a breathing set (204). Learn to clear it in all positions but remember that you now have plenty of air available and can afford to exhale a whole lungful through your nose into your mask if necessary. Remember always to press the part of your mask which is uppermost against your face while allowing the water to be displaced downwards to escape from the bottom edges.

After the novice diver has been trained in these and several other safety drills he will take a proficiency test and progress towards open-water training. During his early training and even more so during his early dives he will appreciate the need for a means of easy communication between divers, which allows them to check their companion's condition, give and receive instructions, warn of dangers, and allow an elementary exchange of information.

203 *Clearing the mouthpiece of a two-stage, single-hose regulator.*

204 *Clearing a mask.*

205 *Swimming practice without a mask.*

206   *A diver with closed-circuit oxygen.*

207

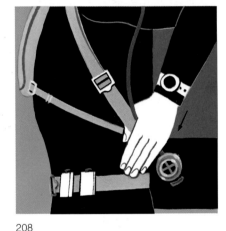

208

Acclimatization training

To begin with, do not go deeper than 10 meters. Only when a diver is perfectly confident at this depth and has mastered the techniques, should he move on to 15 meters in order to prepare for the more extensive dives which are outside the scope of the teaching in this handbook.

There is a point which must be made concerning jumping into the water from a height with partly loose gear such as an inflatable buoyancy jacket or when using two regulators on a double attachment. Jump in with the buoyancy jacket deflated and with the regulator held in the mouth. One hand is on the shoulder straps (207) and also holds the second mouthpiece steady, as well as anything else that is necessary. Nothing must be left hanging loose as it may swing about and hit the diver.

Check that the water is deep enough and beware of landing on top of another diver already in the water. As soon as you are in, test the equipment including the reserve air supply and also the straps of the mask (208).

An important thing to keep in mind at this stage concerns the need to avoid panting and shortness of breath. Normally a person only notices this when it has already started, and will become anxious if it does not disappear immediately after the cause has been rectified.

Therefore it is wise to prevent it from ever starting, which means being able to anticipate when the symptoms are likely to appear. This can be done by using a technique which originated with the use of closed-circuit oxygen breathing apparatus (206) with which shortness of breath was a grave danger. It involves breathing a large volume of air, even though

this means the use of greater physical effort, and taking care to breathe out to the greatest extent. It is therefore a method of breathing based on the principles of hyperventilation. After each inhalation there should be a pause each time of one or two seconds.

The cause of the breathlessness is the carbon dioxide in the system, and when its level rises this pause begins to cause discomfort. This is the alarm signal that warns the diver when breathlessness is approaching. It is only necessary then to eliminate the cause, which is always due to working too hard or inefficiently. At the same time the pauses must be cut out, and the volume of breathing increased, for a few cycles.

This technique should not be employed at a depth where the diver may be approaching his personal limit of resistance to nitrogen narcosis. However, beginners, who are the ones most at risk to the dangers of breathlessness, can use this method at the depths at which they normally operate.

The pause technique uses a great deal of air per cycle which occurs by breathing out to the maximum rather than the reverse. It must not be used when resurfacing because of the increasing volume of air in the lungs, nor during pauses for decompression because it would interfere with the dispersal of nitrogen from the breathing system.

Training for an emergency ascent

The practice routine for a simulated emergency ascent (210) is started at a depth of about 5 meters with the diver on his knees on the seabed breathing deeply in preparation. After a final moderate inhalation, breathe out as much as possible and swim swiftly toward the surface continuing to exhale as you ascend. This should be repeated a number of times until complete confidence is achieved.

The same exercise is then carried out from a depth of 10 meters and is again repeated until complete confidence is gained, and this will come more easily this time. Initial breathing out must be maximum in order to ensure that the increasing volume of air in the lungs never reaches dangerous proportions.

In point of fact emergency ascents under high pressure have been the cause of several accidents even among experienced divers. Although knowledge of the techniques is important practicing them can involve unnecessary risks.

209

210

211 212 *A snorkeler taking air from a diver with SCUBA.*

A faulty valve is not the only cause or even the most dangerous incident which would make an emergency ascent necessary. Trouble can arise from quite simple and unexpected causes. For example, unless he has been trained to think otherwise it would not occur to a diver that there were more than two ways of diving—breathing all the time (SCUBA), or taking a breath at the surface and holding it (snorkel).

A snorkel-diver may go down, even into shallow water, and meet a companion with breathing equipment. Just for fun, he asks him for a mouthful of air (211-212). If he is not prepared, a serious accident could follow. He will actually draw from the regulator a normal free diver's lung-full of air and if he does not exhale as he resurfaces (213) his lungs will over-expand and rupture, even from a depth of as little as 2 or 3 meters.

It is not unusual to hear of such cases. There is, for example, a well-approved training exercise which can be dangerous in this way and yet the risks are seldom pointed out. This is the simulated emergency ascent which is made with two people using the same regulator (215). The vital thing to make clear to the diver is that he must inhale only partially and be ready to breathe out as he ascends.

213   *The snorkeler must exhale as he resurfaces.*

The actions of taking and inserting the mouthpiece, breathing out and in, taking it out again and passing it to one's companion take time and this could mean that the diver is holding his breath for quite a few seconds. Thus, if the speed of ascent is fast, the danger of over-inflation of the lungs is real, especially in the last few meters and is particularly great if one is dealing with a real emergency.

Therefore preparation for this exercise should start with the divers facing each other, shoulder to shoulder at 90° in shal-

214

SCUBA DIVING TECHNIQUES

low water to practice the positions and the movements. The divers share the regulator which passes over the outside shoulder of one of them. Each takes two breaths from the regulator, and holding the second breath passes it to his companion. The diver whose regulator is being used, known as the donor, maintains his grip on the mouthpiece at all times to ensure its eventual return.

The pair should then practice breathing in this same way but standing up. They should stand side by side in what will be their normal position when ascending so that they will not interfere with each other's use of fins. Having gained confidence and rhythm they should try it from 5 meters and when they are entirely perfect at this depth they can continue from 10 meters.

It is important to carry out this exercise carefully and seriously because in a real case of emergency it will not be quite so easy. Some people will try to breathe more than twice, and there have been others who have attacked their helpers. It must be clearly understood that this type of ascent should only be attempted if there is confidence that absolute self-control can be maintained.

It could happen that the signals asking for assistance and for sharing an aqualung might be met with the negative signal. This would mean that each diver must ascend under his own power. A reason for such a refusal would be that it is better to have one diver unconscious and the other able to revive him on the surface than for both to be unconscious and helpless.

In practice today, the use of double regulators and buoyancy compensators means that accidents of this type can now be avoided or reduced to only minor difficulties.

216

Using the buoyancy compensator

The inflatable buoyancy jacket which is used for providing hydrostatic balance is the up-to-date version of the old Mae West, excellent for keeping a man afloat but to be used in an ascent only in desperate cases.

The latest models can be inflated with a small cylinder which is built-in, or by connecting them to the breathing apparatus, or by mouth. They can also be used to provide a few breaths of air which, as can be imagined, could prove very useful at times. Their main use is to maintain hydrostatic balance— so that

weighting and variations of buoyancy can be adjusted as needed. This is most important when diving deep since it allows the diver to adjust his buoyancy at all depths, ensuring complete equilibrium at the bottom and at decompression stops.

It is not altogether easy to get the best out of this item of equipment. Errors of technique could prove awkward so it is necessary to practice some exercises to become familiar with the problems and their solution.

With the buoyancy jacket deflated and weighted for a suitable amount of nega-

tive buoyancy, descend to a sea bottom of not more than 5–10 meters maximum and get into a face-down position. So as not to waste the air in the tank in these first attempts inflate the jacket by mouth until approaching hydrostatic balance (216). Then rise slowly until positive buoyancy begins and, before this becomes excessive, turn head down by rolling forward and return to the bottom. Repeat this many times discovering in this way the maximum degree of positive buoyancy that you can control without letting yourself be dragged involuntarily to the surface.

113

SCUBA DIVING TECHNIQUES

Now try this in slightly deeper water, but this time using either the little internal cylinder of the buoyancy jacket or air from the main breathing tank. When you are approximately in hydrostatic balance swim in circles at the same level with a radius of not more than 10 meters. Then using the same methods as before, and also the exhaust valve on the jacket, change from a state of positive buoyancy to negative buoyancy and repeat this several times.

Use the fin technique which has previously been taught, adjusting the strokes of each leg to maintain the depth and to make the circles. Also, combine with this exercise some practice in using the pause-breathing technique to give warning and control of the onset of breathlessness.

Then take up a kneeling position on the bottom and let more air into the buoyancy compensator. Take out your mouthpiece and breathe in through the tube of the buoyancy jacket. Breathe out through the nose into the water via the mask. Continue letting in gas and breathing in this way but never exhale into the buoyancy jacket, as this could be very dangerous. After this routine has been perfected continue breathing in the same way while concentrating on using the fins correctly and slowly until the surface is reached.

Then go to 10 meters depth, this time using the breathing equipment. Inject air into the buoyancy jacket to give slight positive buoyancy. The increase in the volume of the gas will positively increase the rate of ascent but it will not be as rapid as would be the case in the event of an emergency. Stop your ascent by instantly exhausting the air from the bag so that you become negatively buoyant once more.

Complete this phase by training yourself to walk on the bottom on the hands (217). This is practice for maintaining correct vertical equilibrium which is often necessary during a dive.

217 *Practicing by walking on the hands on the bottom.*

The descent

With negative buoyancy one can descend by sinking. The ideal position, which is also the most comfortable, is like that of a parachutist in free fall (218)—that is, horizontally with the arms and legs spread out. Another way is to remain upright, slowing the descent if necessary with the fins and using them to turn as well if one wants to see all around.

A diver should get used to doing this with the fins alone because his hands may be otherwise occupied. Yet another method is to dive head first, either letting oneself sink naturally or else using the fins.

At the moment of starting the descent the revolving bezel of the watch must be set at zero because as soon as the water pressure is added to the atmospheric pressure nitrogen starts to pass into solution in the tissues. Remember also to clear the ears before the need arises. If there is any difficulty with the pressure compensation routine alternate it with a swallow.

If ear pain occurs it can be eliminated by going back up 1 or 2 meters.

Sometimes one can start in rather muddy water at the surface and find it clear at the bottom and the opposite can also occur. If the visibility at the bottom is inadequate do not go so deep, and if it is still poor at the shallower depths abandon the dive.

Some divers rope themselves together in such cases but this is only to be recommended between two people who get on well with each other. Do not try it with a group of divers as it may happen that one becomes upset and this will have a contagious effect causing trouble for everyone.

218 *A diver 'free-falling' in the background while another pauses on the way up.*

SCUBA DIVING TECHNIQUES

On the bottom

If the bottom is muddy or sandy (219) the fins will disturb the surface and obscure the view. If this is the case it is better to adjust to a slight positive buoyancy which will compel one to swim with the fins higher than the head. Since this attitude will take greater physical effort, hyperventilation and pause-breathing are recommended.

In murky water, apart from the danger of no longer being able to see one's companions even a short distance away, there is always the possibility of becoming entangled in fishing gear (220). Anyone caught like this should remain still to avoid further entanglement and to make it easier for another diver to give aid.

With an irregular bottom one can sometimes move quickly and with a saving in energy by using the hands and arms to pull oneself along (221). This can be very effective without using the flippers and with the body relaxed and the legs and feet trailing.

219 *A sandy bottom must not be disturbed.*

220 *If a diver is caught he should remain still while his buddy cuts him free.*

Remember that limey deposits, shells, sea urchins and the roughness of the rocks can easily cause injuries. A wetsuit gives good protection but unless the water is very cold many divers prefer to work without gloves because the extra sensitivity of touch is invaluable. So get into the habit of first touching lightly in order to feel what you are holding before grasping it or resting on it.

In particular learn to move, to touch, and to enter and leave caves (???) with care so as not to get hurt. Underwater a diver may not notice an injury since the cold acts as an anaesthetic.

After passing through narrow clefts or under overhanging rocks check that the reserve tap, if fitted to your set, is secure because it could have been knocked open.

When entering a tricky passage, or a cave, warn your companion so that he can keep watch without distraction (224). He must always know where you are and what you are doing.

221   *A snorkeler pulling himself along a gully.*

222   *Diving into a cave.*

SCUBA DIVING TECHNIQUES

If you lose sight of your companion do not waste too much time trying to find him. It is better to surface and establish what has happened from there, by looking for his stream of bubbles or his marker buoy with the help of the man in the support boat (223) and so be able to rejoin him directly.

If he is still underwater on his own it could be because he is preoccupied but it might be something worse; the bubbles will clearly show you what has happened. If they arrive in groups at intervals all should be well; if there is a continuous stream of many small bubbles, the other diver may be under an overhanging rock; if, however, large bubbles appear continuously there is cause for alarm.

223 *The safety-boat attendant keeps watch.*

224 *One diver watches while the other works.*

If you have to open your reserve supply you must warn your companion and go up together to a shallower level. Obviously the point at which the reserve will be needed will depend on the capacity of the cylinder, the filling pressure and on individual consumption; so no two people will ever reach this stage simultaneously. The reserve valve must be opened at the first signs of difficulty in inhaling and then you must start ascending immediately.

In a dive like this, one can see how effective and useful signals can be. But they must be limited to essentials because it is not possible to say much in this way and, in any case, there is hardly time to carry on a conversation. The signalling system has been developed as an essential aid and no more.

225 *A pair of divers working together.*

226 *Never go alone into a cave.*

SCUBA DIVING TECHNIQUES

The ascent

When a diver needs to open his reserve, he may find that the valve is too stiff and so he will ask for help, using the appropriate signal.

When he has reached the stage of having to open his reserve or when his instruments indicate that he is approaching (not that he has already reached) the 100 minutes allowed for a dive at not more than 50 feet depth, he must leave the seabed and end the dive. He is then well within the safety curve and if he also stops for a while at between 5 and 3 meters to exhale his remaining air, no danger can arise. One day, however, he may exceed the limit and he will have to wait, hanging onto the boat (see 196 on page 100), even perhaps having to put on a reserve set of breathing equipment. Without this decompression stop he must never go beyond the limits of the safety curve. Many cases of bends have occurred as a result of disregarding this.

Complying with the safety curve and the decompression stops when coming up from a dive are not the only points to watch. It is a major mistake, even if it rarely gives trouble in practice, to come up at too fast a speed. For many years the recommended rate has stood at 18 meters (60 feet) per minute. It is easy to exceed any limit and so, to be on the safe side, let us aim at the speed shown on the decompression tables we are using. Always keep to this speed by using the watch and depth meter.

We already know that speed during the ascent can be dangerous, but slowness can also cause trouble, because unsaturated tissues can continue to absorb nitrogen; this may then exceed the amount laid down as a basis for the decompression tables, which assume that the dive is completed at the moment when the ascent starts.

Ascending with the anchor cable as a guide will simplify things, but this is not always possible. Therefore, practice dealing with a less simple situation and learn to recognize the correct speed instinctively. Compare it with the speed of ascent of the bubbles (228). This speed must never be exceeded (227).

An emergency ascent

The importance of knowing about this cannot be overstated. At the depths we have been considering, and with sufficient knowledge and training, a diver can surface without any particular difficulty unless he is ill or suffers some accident.

Therefore the cases that concern us most are those due to an unexpected illness (unlikely at these depths if the diver is fit and well-trained), or the complete failure of the regulator, or else because of some accident aggravated by the depth, or by panic or shortage of breath. If anything goes seriously wrong it can nearly always be signalled to a companion provided contact and attention has been maintained. Often the helper can be guided with the correct signals and even those few which are internationally accepted give a reasonable range of choice.

A faulty valve is no longer the dramatic incident it was in the past. If the dive has been properly organized, and if the equipment is complete, either the double regulator or the possibility of breathing air from the small cylinder of the buoyancy jacket (229) or the regulator of one's diving companion (230) will usually solve the problem, provided a little self-control is maintained. This way the extreme solution of a buoyant ascent can be avoided, because this can be very dangerous, especially when the dive is outside the limits of the safety curve.

If there is no double regulator available and if the situation is serious the procedure is to release the weight belt so that it falls away. But do not remove the breathing apparatus, as the regulator may resume working and in any case the advantage to be gained in being relieved of the burden will not compensate for the energy expended in freeing oneself from it.

Shortage of air due to an empty tank cannot now be considered an accident. When the diver is breathing calmly and then interrupts his dive at the first sign of difficulty, an ascent is no problem. For every 10 meters covered the pressure is reduced by 1 atmosphere and, due to

229

230

expansion, several liters become available which are continually augmented as he approaches the surface.

Anyone whose dive is outside the limits of the safety curve, however, faces major risks in the event of an emergency ascent.

It must be repeated that when breathing during the ascent, do not breathe in too fully. Pause-breathing must not be used, and the rate of breathing must be normal. If there is some doubt that due to the time factor or to the depth or because of the nature of the work being carried out, one is close to the limit of the safety curve, a stop of at least 5 minutes at 5 meters is essential. However, this type of case will be dealt with later.

The safety boat

The boat is the diver's home base and he should always find it close at hand when he surfaces (231). Propellers should only be operated with care above men who are diving. Large motorboats and other craft which cannot be maneuvered easily should only be used when anchored and divers are therefore restricted to remaining very close to the anchorage. In order to follow the divers' movements a small boat is needed, preferably with oars or an outboard motor, and which can also hoist the divers' warning flag to prevent other boats approaching. It must be big enough to hold the diving party plus all the equipment and baggage and must have good stability. The boatman

must be experienced with divers, be able to follow a submerged swimmer and be able to understand divers' signals.

In following a diver the boat should be kept within 20 meters of the diver's bubbles or marker buoy (232). Never put the boat immediately above divers because this would be dangerous in the event of an emergency ascent. And never lose sight of them. When the sea is choppy this is not easy; other passengers must not get in the way or rock the boat or obstruct the man in charge. Following bubbles in anything but the calmest conditions is unlikely to be successful and the use of a diver's marker buoy is strongly recommended.

Once contact with the bubbles is lost,

231 *Divers working with a base boat.*

due perhaps to wind or current, the distance between the submerged men and the boat may become considerable. In a rough sea it can be difficult not only to see the bubbles but even to spot a man on the surface. So divers should always have a whistle so that they can be heard at a distance. A surfacing diver may not be able to see the boat due to the color and shape of the coast behind or to fog and this could be serious if he is exhausted or in trouble. The snorkel-diver is constantly returning to the surface and knows very well where he is in relation to the boat. The SCUBA-diver, on the other hand, is under water a long time and does not know where he will finish up when he emerges and what he will find

on the surface. Also his breathing equipment, when exhausted, becomes a dead weight and impedes his swimming.

The safety-boat must be kept tidy and all the equipment ready for use. Anything vulnerable to getting wet should be stowed in the bow. Empty cylinders must be easily distinguishable and separated from full ones and each diver must keep his own equipment together and not scattered around. If groups of divers are going down in turn, the second group should prepare themselves only after the first group has left everything in order.

Anyone who suffers from seasickness must be careful because diving could make it worse. This will be particularly likely when the bottom is covered with

waving weeds such as eel grass. Remember that an attack of vomiting while diving can be very awkward, especially for someone who is deep and cannot surface in time.

If it proves difficult to obtain a safety-boat you should not take the easy way out and make do with a diver's marker buoy alone. If something goes wrong a buoy can never be as useful as a boat! Take care also that the depth and the nature of the sea bottom do not allow the mooring line to become tangled or caught in among rocks because this would limit the freedom of movement of the safety-boat.

Surfacing

If a diver surfaces some distance from his support boat on account of having misjudged the current or because the boatman was at fault, a successful pick-up could depend on the integral buoyancy of the wet-suit. The diver should inflate his buoyancy jacket and indicate to the boatman whether he wishes to be picked up or if he intends to swim to the boat using his fins. He can swim on his back or on his front using his snorkel. To cover a long distance, however, he may have to discard his breathing equipment and anything else which will impede his progress.

Trainee divers who stick to the rules and are prepared to follow the advice of the more experienced will never get into such a situation. Also, they will never be without a whistle, an inflatable buoyancy-jacket and a snorkel. It is only those who think they are more expert than they actually are, who will dive without such aids. The good SCUBA-diver knows that the sea is always stronger than man and must be treated with intelligence, with caution, and with the right techniques.

When coming out one can take off some equipment in the water. If, in an emergency, it is necessary to drop heavy equipment which will sink, it would be well to retain the mask to the end in order to see. It is nice to be able to lighten oneself to prevent fatigue but not if one has to dive again immediately to recover it. The only rule is that when one is climbing into a small boat the fins are a help and should therefore be removed afterwards. If the boat has a ladder then it will be better to take the fins off.

Although dives may be planned to be within the limits of the safety curve, errors or accidents may still happen. Because of this it is essential for all divers to know where the nearest decompression chamber is and the quickest way of getting to it. This is the first question to ask on arriving at a new location, or even before leaving home.

Depth limitations

Having now covered the practical training of a diver including his equipment, the descent, compensation and behavior underwater, we will only refer to these subjects again if it is necessary to do so to complete some other explanation. Also for the moment we will not concern ourselves with the automatic decompression meter but will get into the habit of consulting the watch and the depth gauge to become accustomed to the necessary calculations.

The normal depth of a dive is about 50 feet which is within the safety curve. If diving in experienced company it is possible to make descents in the region of 75 feet. A beginner should never attempt to dive to his personal maximum depth without first exploring the water beneath the surface to gain confidence.

At 50 feet it is possible to remain for a maximum of 100 minutes without passing outside the limits of the safety curve. This is a long time and from many points of view it is more rewarding than going much deeper where one could remain only a few minutes. Do not imagine that to get the most out of a dive one has to go deep. Just as is the case on land, finding beauty is not always predictable. The sea bottom is very different in different places and will vary with the time of day from early dawn to dusk. When enough experience is gained to allow night diving in clear waters, especially those rich in plankton, there will be incredible landscapes to admire even over bottoms which are normally monotonous stretches of sand.

234 *Divers feeding fish.*

Diving signals

The member countries of the World Underwater Federation (CMAS) have adopted a basic set of hand-signals which are in use by many thousands of divers all around the world. The set includes signals to be made at the surface for communication between two divers, or between a diver and his boat or shore party, and also signals to be used between divers when underwater, including questions and answers, instructions on direction and position, and warnings of danger or emergency.

Some signals are shown here which are in use only in the U.S.

The signals should be learned at the beginning of training and used regularly so that they are instantly understood in an emergency.

235
OK, all is well.
Are you OK?
(*US - UK - Europe*)

236
Go up.
I am going up.
(*US - UK - Europe*)

237
Go down.
I am going down.
(*US - UK - Europe*)

238
I am on reserve.
I have 30/50 ATS remaining.
(*US - UK - Europe*)

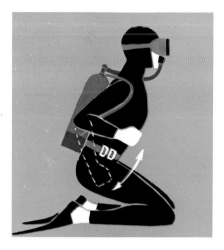

239
I cannot open my reserve.
Open my reserve.
(*US - UK - Europe*)

240
I am in trouble.
(*Europe*)

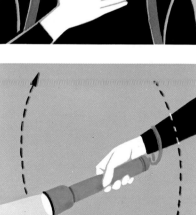

241
Danger.
Help me.
(*Europe*)

242
At surface -
I am in trouble.
Help me.
(*Europe*)

243
At night -
OK, all is well.
(*US - UK - Europe*)

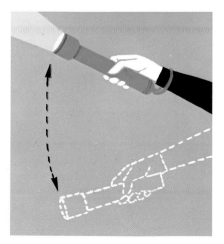

244
At night -
All is not well.
(*US - UK - Europe*)

127

245
Me.
The following signal refers to me.
(*Europe*)

246
You or me
(pointing).
(*US - UK - Europe*)

247
You or me
(pointing slowly).
(*Europe*)

248
Assemble here.
(*US - UK - Europe*)

249
Stop.
Stay where you are.
(*US - UK - Europe*)

250
Direction indicated.
(*US - UK - Europe*)

251
No.
I cannot
It is wrong.
(*Europe*)

252
Slow down.
Relax.
(*US - UK - Europe*)

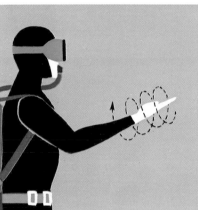

253
Hurry up.
(*Europe*)

254
Adjust.
(*Europe*)

255
I don't understand.
Repeat.
(*Europe*)

256
I am slightly dizzy.
(*Europe*)

257
Something is wrong
but not an emergency.
(*US - UK*)

258
I am out of breath.
(*US - UK*)

259
I have no more air.
(*US - UK*)

260
Distress.
I need immediate assistance.
(*US - UK*)

261
A line is to be made fast.
(*often used when lifting an object
from the sea bottom*)
(*US - UK - Europe*)

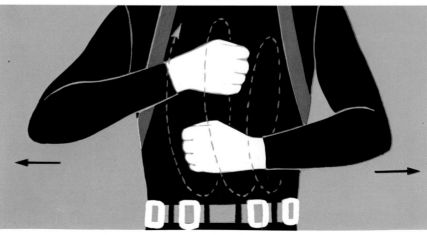

262
Danger.
Danger there (point).
(*US UK*)

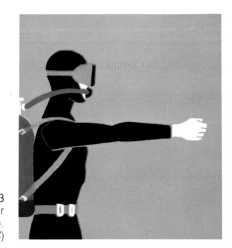

263
Danger
(fist points to danger).
(*US*)

264
At surface -
OK, all is well.
(*US - UK*)

265
At surface -
OK.
(*US*)

266
At surface -
Distress.
Come and get me.
(*US - UK*)

267
At surface -
OK.
(*US*)

Knots

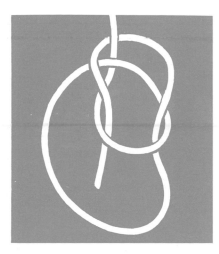

Anyone going in for underwater sport must know certain basic knots:

268
Bowline
*(A quickly made loop.
This knot never jams
and can always be easily untied,
but is completely secure under load)*

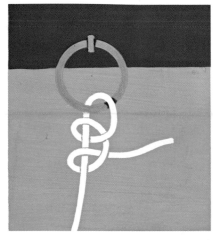

269
**Half-turn and
two half-hitches**
*(For securing a line
to a ring or bar)*

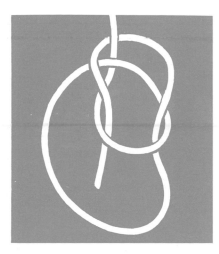

270
Clove hitch
*(A simple way of fastening a line,
especially for a temporary mooring)*

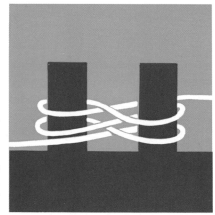

271
Belaying
*(To make a line fast to a bollard
or cleat so that it can easily be
cast off. Use alternate cross-over
turns)*

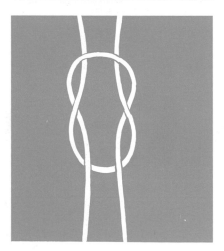

272
Reef or square knot
*(For joining two lines
of nearly equal size)*

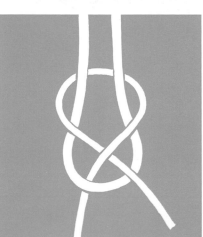

273
Sheet bend
*(For joining two lines
of unequal size.
Also for joining a line
to a loop or eye)*

274 to 277 *Divers working from an underwater pressure chamber.*

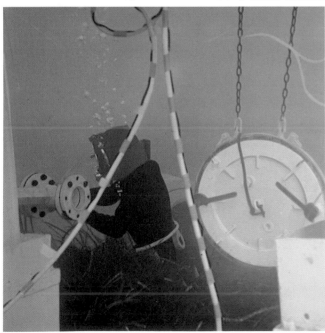

278 *Preparing for an ice dive.*

PART

4

The
Dangers
and the
Rewards

Accidents and first aid

279 *Anemone.*

The possibilities

The most serious diving accidents, and the ones continually to be on the watch for, have already been discussed. They can occur in combinations which make it difficult to decide on the correct treatment unless specific training has been given. However, there is no doubt that the most useful, and the simplest, form of first aid is artificial respiration.

There are many other types of possible accident, some well known, and some pretty unlikely. There are the sort of things which can happen to anyone on dry land as well as others more or less frightening which can be met in certain waters. There are species of sharks, for example, which are sometimes aggressive in certain circumstances. There are snakes which are not aggressive, but do, however, carry a lethal poison. There are certain fish and shells which have poisonous spines, and there are the familiar sea urchins which frequently cause minor injury to a diver, either because there are a lot of them or because he does not notice and bumps against them.

Let us look for a start at only the most simple of accidents and those that call for immediate first aid.

280 *Don't touch a jellyfish!*

281 *A worm.*

282 *Bristle worms.*

283 *Stone fish.*

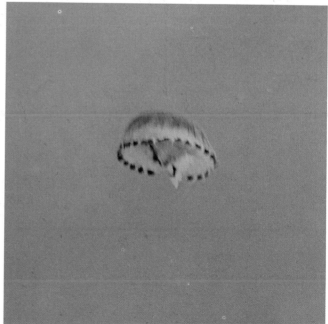

284 *Jellyfish.*

137

Resuscitation

Wounds, fractures, burns and even an embolism can wait for a while. On the other hand, resuscitation cannot, even for a few seconds.

In most cases it is easy to recognize when artificial respiration is needed (285, 286, 287); the method is not difficult and is effective. In a case of loss of consciousness, for example, a diver can give first aid easily and without risk. First check if the victim is breathing or not. If he is breathing it is a case of blackout and he can be left to breathe fresh air. Dry and warm him if he is cold, raise his legs higher than his head if he is pale, and protect him from the sun if he is hot.

Of course the actual cause of the collapse may be serious, but there is nothing more than can be done on the spot. However, even simple first aid is effective in at least 90 per cent of the cases.

On the other hand, the accidents which inevitably threaten the life of the victim are those that involve the breathing system or, worse still, the heart. We know by now what can happen in this new environment. First there is the typical suffocation of drowning which can affect divers with SCUBA gear through flooding of the regulator or other complications. Then we have various types of unconsciousness of differing origins which could be voluntary or involuntary, simple or complicated. These result from holding the breath too long or from hyperventilation, in which more or less the first obvious symptom is the stoppage in breathing. We then have the anoxia syncope which affects both the breathing and the heart. There are also the cases where the heart has stopped beating owing to delay in rescue, either because of suffocation or during a free-diving blackout.

285   *The snorkeler is unconscious.*

287 *Rescue using an inflatable ring.*

286 *Rescuing an unconscious diver.*

288 *Rescue from a helicopter.*

139

Artifical respiration

If breathing has stopped, air must be supplied to the lungs. This is done by means of artificial respiration. If there is more than only a few minutes delay serious brain damage or death may already have occurred.

Success is not difficult to achieve provided the victim is discovered immediately after the accident. Artificial respiration should be attempted even after a delay of 15 minutes, but the longer the interval the more likely it is that the heart will also have stopped.

The various tests and preparations recommended by some authorities before starting treatment are desirable but not essential. The really urgent action is to force some air into the lungs, even briefly, as soon as possible. The most commonly used system today is 'mouth-to-mouth' resuscitation.

A precise position for the body cannot be laid down because the conditions and circumstances vary so much. The important thing is that the chin should be fully extended (290) because in this position the tongue will be prevented from slipping back and blocking the air passages (289).

Two possible positions are shown in the illustrations (291, 292). The rescuer blows in air and then allows it to escape; this can best be done by placing his mouth over the mouth or nose of the patient (293). If the mouth is kept open the nose is pinched closed (294). It is important that the air should really go in and not escape. This can be seen by

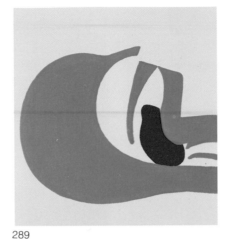

289

290

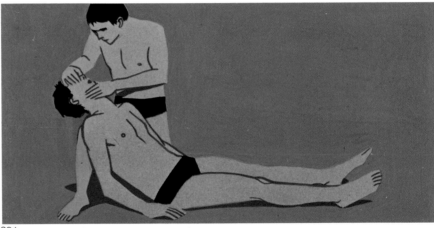

291

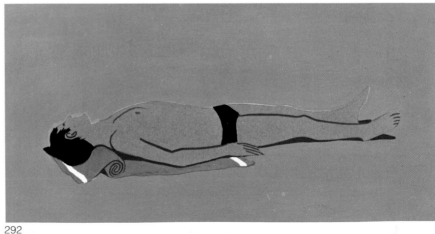

292

watching the upper part of the chest, which should rise and fall.

Start by giving several quick puffs, and then the rhythm should be slowed to 10–12 per minute. It is possible to exhale a considerable volume of air into the victim's lungs, which is not pure air, but the act of artificial respiration leads to a certain amount of hyperventilation on the part of the rescuer; this automatically raises the percentage of oxygen in the air which is inflating the lung pockets.

For some, mouth-to-mouth is not a particularly pleasant method, but there are special plastic tubes available which avoid the need for direct contact with the mouth of the patient. One can also use the rubber tube from some types of breathing sets.

The mouth-to-mouth system should not be attempted when, as often happens, the breathing passages are flooded. This will be shown by froth at the mouth which can be white, red or pink. Hopefully this accident will have taken place in the sea, because salt water is richer in salt than is blood and does not diffuse beyond the lining of the lungs. Fresh water, not containing salt, diffuses into the tissues and into the blood by the osmosis process and will reduce the chances of recovery.

The patient will be on his back, which is fine for carrying out heart massage if this becomes necessary, but is no good for getting rid of the water. So turn him face down in order to use one of the other methods of manual artificial respiration (295).

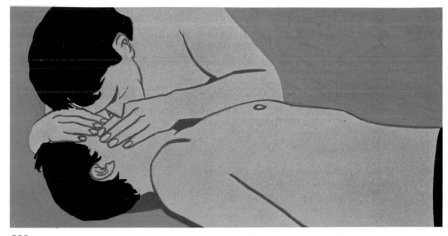

293

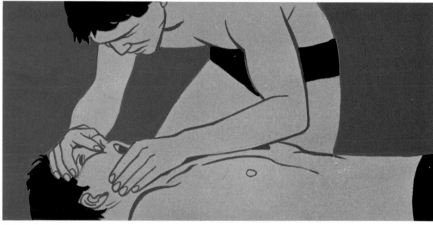

294

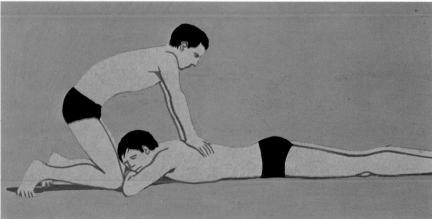

295

These methods do not allow liquids to enter the lungs, but pump them into the throat and so towards the exit. Their action is to work the chest like bellows from the outside, unlike the mouth-to-mouth system which inflates the chest from the inside. Ventilation is therefore with pure air in this case.

The most efficient method of this type is the Holger-Nielsen, which pumps a volume of about 1 liter each time (296). It can be combined with the Schafer method when two operators are available (299).

Again, after a few quick cycles, reduce the rhythm to about 12 respirations per minute. Each should be about 5 seconds total, of which 2 seconds are for the exhalation, which is forced and rapid, and 3 seconds for the inhalation, which is partly spontaneous and therefore slower.

Generally the patient should be lying flat with the head slightly lower, the hands placed beneath the temples and with the chin extended (296).

The rescuer should kneel and work by moving his weight forwards and backwards, always with the arms fully stretched. Keep time by counting from one to five and starting with the hands below the shoulder blades, fingers outwards—the position at the end of the pressure phase.

From one to three the arms slide off the shoulder blades onto the arms and then grip the elbows. These are swung towards the operator without being lifted but are simply brought forward, bringing them closer together (297). The effect is to raise the ribs more without moving the patient's hands from under his head. Then return to the pressure position which is reached at five, and press downward.

Take care that the application of pressure is even and not too great, or broken ribs may easily be the result. The same danger is also present with heart massage. Because of this danger it is wise always to use the mouth-to-mouth method with children, and small adults.

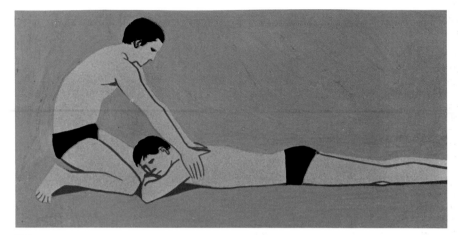

296

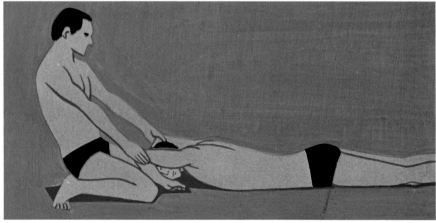

297

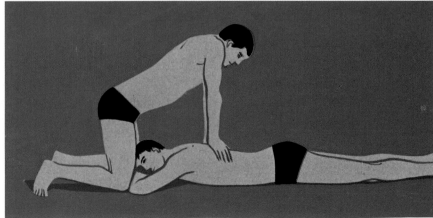

298

Heart massage

It is not always too easy to be sure if the heart is beating because of other noises or because of the unavoidable anxiety in the helpers, or because the heart beats are too weak.

The best way to find out if the heart is still beating is to place one's ear on the chest (301). Another way is to feel the carotid artery, rather than the wrist pulse which is too indefinite (300); the illustration shows how.

In a case of doubt it is better to act, but this would not be so for artificial respiration. In fact if the victim is still breathing, artificial methods might oppose the natural breathing and this could be fatal. On the other hand with a very weak and rapid heart beat even if some strokes are out of phase this will not be continuous and the odds are that most will be of positive help. We can, therefore, say that if by mistake we try to stimulate a heart that is beating feebly there should not be any danger.

To carry out heart massage (302) the rescuer should place his hands on top of each other on the lower part of the breast bone of the victim. Press down firmly on the area of the chest, which will stimulate the heart; then lift up again at a rate of about 40 compressions per minute. As can be seen this could be harmful and do serious damage if applied with too much force, therefore it must be carried out with great care.

With all methods of resuscitation two points must be borne in mind: the urgency of acting and the perseverance in prolonging it. Do not be discouraged. Hope must be sustained for a long time. There have been cases of survival even after hours of work on a victim! Do not give in to fatigue; you can change position or even change the method.

Embolism

In all cases of embolism including 'bends' or decompression sickness the best treatment is recompression in a pressure chamber with absolute rest while waiting for it to disappear. Certain drugs may be prescribed in some cases and oxygen breathing equipment should be available

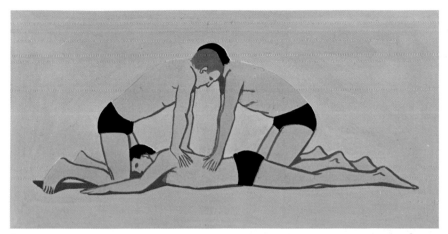

299

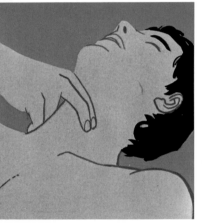

300

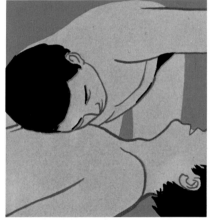

301

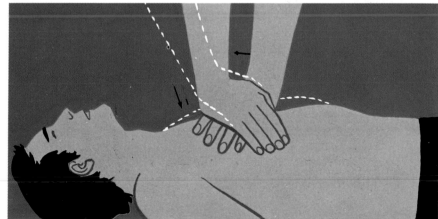

302

with which the patient can breathe for some hours if necessary if there should be a delay in getting him to a pressure chamber.

Recompression by taking the victim down again into the water should be left to professional divers or to specialist medical teams. As an emergency solution it is not suitable for various reasons. It can give good results if the decompression in water is carried out for some hours, even by night if necessary, while a boat runs a shuttle service to replenish the breathing equipment of the patient and his helpers. However, success in such cases is extremely rare.

Nitrogen narcosis

Compared to an embolism, which in normal amateur diving usually shows up on the surface as a case of decompression sickness or 'bends', nitrogen narcosis is more dangerous because it occurs deep down. One good thing about it is that by rising from deep water it automatically disappears but if unchecked in this way, the condition will get worse, and one can even reach a stage of losing consciousness while in a state of narcosis. This, of course, will be fatal if a potential rescuer does not spot it.

When helping in such a case it is important not to let the victim lose his mouthpiece, because he is breathing and otherwise would suffocate. If help comes in time the process of rising to a lesser depth will allow the victim to recover, and even if the dive is outside the limits of the safety curve, he will be able to make the normal stops for decompression.

If he has lost his mouthpiece (303) it is best to hold his head with the chin stretched out. Ascend like this and the expanding air will be released.

303 *If the diver has lost his mouthpiece, keep his chin extended.*

A burst eardrum

The immediate effects have already been described, and the after treatment is simple. In about ten days at the most, provided care is taken, the eardrum will heal on its own just like any other tissue.

Apart from the treatment advised by a specialist, who should always be consulted, it is advisable not to blow one's nose. If it cannot be avoided, only blow one side at a time leaving the other nostril completely open and use as little force as possible.

The aim is to avoid the pressure passing up the Eustachian tube to the middle ear and re-opening the wound. This would delay recovery and jeopardize the complete healing of the membrane.

Muscle cramp

Cramp can be caused by bruising but it is generally due to cold and also to fatigue when a diver is out of training.

The muscles affected are generally those of the legs and the feet. They contract, causing pain, and make further movement impossible (304). Ordinary swimmers are afraid of cramp, though it is not likely that it would be serious, and it is not normally a problem that worries the diver.

If it should occur, relax and massage the joint, while trying to overcome the contraction of the muscle by stretching it. For example, if it is affecting the calf muscle in the leg, stretch it out, grasp the end of the flipper and pull.

Dangerous marine animals

There is a distinction between those that attack, which are very few, those that bite when they are disturbed or injured, and those that one only needs to avoid, which are by far the most numerous. To catalog them all would be impossible and of little practical help. Local divers and fishermen can tell one what to beware of.

Sharks are the traditional enemies of man but very few are aggressive, and these are usually confined to limited areas. Most sharks are cowardly when alone or in small groups and do not attack spontaneously. They are not often roused, especially if the object appears to them to be harmless.

304 *A diver with cramp is brought to the surface.*

On the other hand, a school of sharks can be dangerous. In some areas shark attacks are frequent; they do not need to be very large for their danger to be very great. However, their bite is not very powerful in proportion to their size. The conger eel, the moray eel (309) and the *orato*, or parrot fish can all exert more force. The shark's teeth are movable and their bite does not cut, it lacerates. It is perhaps because of this that some people have been saved after a shark attack. When meeting a shark of dubious intent it is better to turn to face it while retreating toward a boat or the shore or other shelter. One can then watch it and take advantage of its natural cowardice; this attitude often succeeds.

Even today, not much is known about shark behavior, but there are some general rules to keep in mind when in shark territory. Do not wear bright clothes. These seem to pique their curiosity. Remove wounded fish immediately; do not keep them in a diver's bag. Do not swim at night. But always remember: danger in a shark attack is much rarer than is popularly believed, so don't panic.

Animals that inject poisons of greater or lesser danger range from shellfish like the coneshell to fish like the weever fish (*trachinoidei*) or the sea scorpion (*scorpenodei*) or to animals like the long spined sea urchin of warm seas. Nor should we forget bites such as those of the slightly poisonous octopus or the less likely bites of the snake whose poison can be more potent than that of the king cobra. Finally it is as well to remember also the jagged weapon of certain species of ray (307) which is covered with a poisonous mucus. This is a bone in the tail which the animal violently lashes around when it feels itself in danger.

Injuries from contact with some fish result in an electric shock which one can get from one of the ray species, the electric ray, as well as from a species of eel, the electric eel.

The offensive apparatus of the stinging animals is made up of thousands of cells which are each like a microscopic

305 *Hunters with a turtle.*

306 *Lionfish.*

injecting needle or alternatively have very fine spikes which embed themselves in the skin. The animal and vegetable covering of the rocky walls (308) or the coral growths of warmer waters are only slightly irritant, except for the so-called fire coral which is exceedingly so. Irritation will be felt if bare skin is in contact for a short time. If one were to harpoon a large fish and drag it across a bed of coral the skin would be scraped off and sometimes the flesh as well.

There are also dangerous stinging animals of which the worst is the Portuguese Man o'war, which can be so painful as to cause a man to black out. This is an extreme case; the stings of other jelly fish or sea anemones are less troublesome.

The first aid for deep bites is to check the bleeding, as with ordinary wounds, with a pad or a tourniquet (311) making sure that the circulation is not stopped for more than 15-20 minutes at a time. Hydrogen peroxide is very good for cleaning and disinfecting a wound.

307 *Stingray*

308 *Anemone.*

309 *Moray eel.*

147

ACCIDENTS AND FIRST AID

The symptoms associated with injury from animals that inject venom are pain, reddening, bluish coloring and swelling. The patient may also show weakness, vomiting, diarrhea, collapse and paralysis. Recommendations are to suck and squeeze the place immediately and to open up the wound in order to get rid of as much poison as possible. Get medical help as quickly as possible.

To reduce the pain it is helpful to apply very hot or very cold compresses according to the circumstances. If available, pain-killers can be given. Stimulants which will help to reverse the initial collapse can be administered by medical personnel.

The symptoms of contact with stinging animals are immediate pain and burning. The skin is reddened and becomes inflamed and there can be nausea, vomiting, paralysis and even delirium in the most serious cases such as those with Portuguese Man o'war. The severity of the effects depends also on the particular species, the size of the area affected and the length of the time of contact. Treatment indicated includes pain-killers, local cleaning with a mild antiseptic solution, antihistamine, cortisone and antibiotic ointments.

Especially in waters where these dangers are more common it is advisable to be prepared for the occasion. A first-aid box can contain the medicines mentioned as well as a tourniquet, syringes ready for use, at least two vials of heart stimulants, analgesic tablets, cortisone ointment for reducing inflammation, antibiotic ointment, tweezers for extracting spines, bandages, sterile gauze, adhesive tape, decongestants, anti-seasickness tablets and eye ointment.

310 *Learn which animals to avoid.*

311 *Applying a tourniquet.*

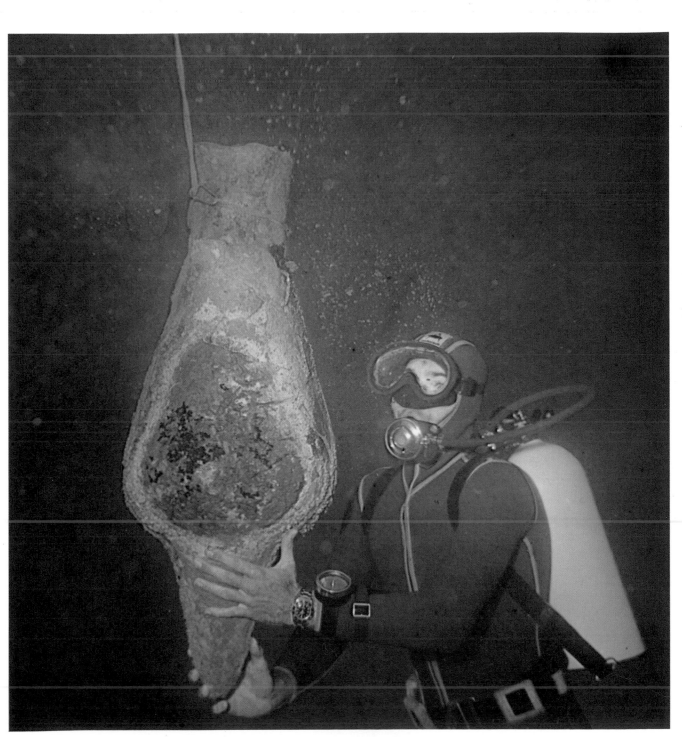

312 *Lifting an amphora from an archaeological site.*

Using one's skills

313 *A spear-fisherman.*

Competition

The first competitive international activity was underwater hunting (313) which was followed by fin swimming (which is really a surface activity) and then by SCUBA techniques. There is little formal competition in the United States, but in Europe it is growing, as the Mediterranean coast of France was the birthplace of the sport.

Underwater competition, however, is still not large in terms of numbers taking part and so the chances of doing well are good. This is an attraction for young enthusiasts who frequently can reach national, international and world championship standards.

The underwater fisherman (314) does not learn in the formal way, as is usual in sports today, with an instructor and a trainer. Each goes fishing for his own entertainment and becomes his own teacher by trial and error. It is a form of athletic competition which allows a man to train while enjoying himself. It is a painless method but undoubtedly has some risk.

Diving technique is the common point of contact between pure sport, science and technological progress. Technique means speed, orientation, adequate experience of underwater behavior, special skills and so on.

314 *A hunter with a speared grouper.*

To set out the principles of diving is not particularly exciting but underneath the bare description of the techniques we find a world bubbling with new ideas and applications (315).

For example, in the field of equipment the compasses that we have today could be used to steer a trans-atlantic liner; divers are now able to have distance meters more accurate than a motor car's; there is equipment that gives his depth to the nearest centimeter. The Russians are apparently even experimenting with a special type of radar for divers.

Even though diving can never be a spectator sport, there is no doubt that for young people in search of new fields to conquer it is a challenge well worth considering—and it might lead to great things. For example, in tomorrow's world an expert in instrumental navigation capable of working to great accuracy in water of zero visibility would be a valuable asset. And do not forget: the marine world is man's last unexplored frontier.

315 *Getting ready for the competition.*

316 *Competition fins.*

317 *Competition mono-fin.*

In competitive swimming with fins, the Italians were supreme in the early years but have now lost their lead. Due to innovations in their equipment the Russians, both men and women came to the fore. Later they showed that their supremacy did not depend only on their equipment, but also on the adoption of interval-training, which allowed a considerable increase in the length and width of their fins (316) followed by the introduction of the mono fin (317) which is flipped like a dolphin's tail for speed events.

It is only recently that the sport of fin swimming has begun to produce its own specialized athletes. They came to it first by way of normal swimming, but this new sport requires a totally different approach from the crawl, where the legs produce only 30 per cent of the effort. Fin racers need to develop muscles which give all the thrust from the legs. Thus the development of underwater competition is still wide open to young athletes prepared to learn and become familiar with its special needs and some day fin swimming could be an Olympic sport.

Recreation

Enough has been said to show that underwater, not only those who enter competitions, but recreational divers also, have to take the sport seriously. The latter may not be so muscular and are perhaps less frequent practitioners but they are just as

318

319 *The diver enjoys being at home with the fish.*

much subject to the rigid discipline which is the result of their special knowledge and abilities. Without this concentration on efficiency, preparedness and self-control, any diver is exposed to considerable risk.

Just being underwater is the basis of the sport and is still the only aim of many of the participants. As soon as he drops below the surface a diver is cut off from the everyday world so completely that, even if he did nothing more, he could find himself fully satisfied (319). It can hold him in its spell like a dream which dissolves and vanishes as soon as he resurfaces.

320 *Using an aquaplane towed by a boat.*

USING ONE'S SKILLS

At first simple snorkel-diving attracted underwater sightseers and was the origin of all subsequent developments. It started with fetching souvenirs from the bottom or collecting specimens for early underwater naturalists who had realized the possibilities of this method of selection instead of blanket dredging (322).

This led to the plunder of trophies taken from the sea which then were displayed in people's homes. Nowadays shells, which were the currency of earlier times, have regained their value and amphorae have attracted the looters and this has aroused the concern of archaeologists. Today, a diver must learn to respect the ecology of the sea.

322 *Diver with a starfish and a sea urchin.*

321 *Preparing to lift a lead anchor stock with an air bag.*

323 *Using a lifting bag on an ancient anchor.*

The lure of caves has enticed the diver to extend his activities to underground water with special equipment and preparation (324, 325). The sea diver has a clear route to the surface in case of danger but the cave explorer has a much more difficult task. He must retrace his route in order to get back and is subject to the psychological effects of claustrophobia, which are all the more pronounced in an alien environment.

324 *Divers entering a cave.*

325 *Diving in an underwater lake.*

USING ONE'S SKILLS

Another aspect of the sport is photographing and filming for fun or to record scenes for painters or to reconstruct at home some small part of underwater life (326, 327, 328). From the study of how to recreate the environment and maintain conditions which will sustain life have grown the techniques of the aquarium, which is a valuable source of interest, observation and study. It has been possible, for example, to transfer red coral from great depth to an aquarium and keep it alive (330).

The search for new specimens and then studying how to capture and recover them without damage, requires not only considerable diving skills but also a love of nature and a great deal of time and enthusiasm.

The marine world is full of life and wonder; a whole new universe opens up for those who are ready to explore. It is, in fact, one of the last frontiers of our planet.

326 *A tropical seawater aquarium.*

327 *Underwater photography.*

328 *Filming underwater.*

329 *Divers play with an octopus.*

330 *Collecting specimens on a cliff face.*

Appendix

ADDRESSES

The two largest U.S. Associations are:
National Association of Underwater Instructors (NAUI)
4650 Arrow Highway, Suite F-1, Montclair, CA 91763, (714) 621-5801
Professional Association of Diving Instructors (PADI)
1251 East Dyer Road, #100, Santa Ana, CA 92705, (714) 540-7234
Both offer diving courses and have numerous regional and local affiliates
throughout the country and abroad.

Other useful addresses:
Confederation Mondiale des Activites Subaquatiques (CMAS)
World Underwater Federation, 47 rue du Commerce, 75015 Paris, France
A full list of the affiliated national Associations is obtainable from CMAS. Among them:
Underwater Society of America (USA)
P.O. Box 628, Daly City, CA, (415) 583-8492
National YMCA SCUBA Program
Oakbrook Square, 6083-A Oakbrook Parkway, Norcross, GA 30093
Federazione Italiana Pesca Sportiva (FIPS)
Viale Tiziano 70, 00196 Rome, Italy
F.C.A.S.
5334 Yonge Street, Suite 208, Toronto, Ontario M2N 6M2, Canada
Australian Underwater Federation
P O Box 1006, Civic Square, Canberra Act 2608, Australia
CMAS Dive Club
c/o Mr Farrelly Warren, P O Box 4137, Whangarei, New Zealand

SOME METRIC MEASUREMENTS AND THEIR U.S. EQUIVALENTS

LENGTH

1 centimeter	=	0.393 inches
1 meter	=	3.280 feet
1 kilometer	=	0.621 miles

WEIGHT

1 gram	=	0.035 ounce
1 kilogram	=	2.205 pounds
1 metric ton	=	2,205 pounds

VOLUME

1 cubic centimeter	=	0.061 cubic feet
1 cubic meter	=	35.314 cubic feet
1 liter (1000 cc)	=	0.035 cubic feet
1 liter	=	0.220 gallons

PRESSURE

1 kilogram per square centimeter	=	14.223 pounds per square inch
1 atmosphere	=	14.7 pounds per square inch

Index

Index